Letters From Prison

Letters From Prison

NAN BRADLEY

ARPress

ILLUMINATING IDEAS.
EMPOWERING VOICES

ARPress
45 Dan Road Suite 5
Canton MA 02021
Hotline: 1(888) 821-0229
Fax: 1(508) 545-7580

Ordering Information:
Quantity sales.Special discounts are available on quantity purchases by corporations, associations, and others.For details, contact the publisher at the address above.

Printed in the United States of America.

ISBN-13:   Softcover   979-8-89330-845-7
                  eBook   979-8-89330-846-4

Library of Congress Control Number: 2024902466

INTRODUCTION

Don't look at me like that! Don't judge me because I've been in prison. You don't know me; you don't know the terrible thing that happened to send me to prison. I'm not a bad person. I didn't rob anybody. I didn't rape anybody; I didn't get your kids on drugs. I'm a good person with a big loving heart.

Here is my story. You may believe it or not but it's true, and an eye-opening experience. It could happen to you or your children. God got me through this but without him I would have been lost. The first time I knew God was real was when I was ten years old. I got a knife that I loved for Christmas. I lost it and was heartbroken. A few weeks later, I was walking down a gravel rock when a voice whispered in my ear.

"Stop, Look down at your feet! I looked down and there was my Knife. I knew God was real and was talking to me. I'm so glad I was listening.

LETTERS FROM PRISON

I came from a two-week fishing trip and was cooking fish, when someone banged on my door and shouted! "Open up, this is police!" They had a search warrant and found that in the back of the house, fans were on, and they could still tell someone had been cooking. I explained that I knew nothing about it and that I had to been on a fishing trip out of state. They said, "We know who did it, we have been hiding in the woods outside, waiting to catch him. When you pulled up, he made his escape. We are going back on stakeout for a few days waiting to see if he returns."

They arrested me and took me to jail with no bail. The older man that I was fishing saw the news with the story of my arrest and a picture of me. He came to jail, and they let me go after he swore, I was with him. My mom was at my house when I got home. Lots ff policeman where there. They were going thru the trash and looking for anything they could find to tie me to the lab that was inside my house. My mom ask, "What is happening?" The officer told her but explained that they knew I had no knowledge to what happened. They knew who did it. He had left the country and as far as they could figure out, he went to Russia.

Life continued for a couple of months I hired a lawyer. He tried to get me probation. The police said if I could give them some drugs deals to make an arrest, they would drop the charges. My mom and I tried to find drugs and buy so we could give the police some leads, hoping they could make an arrest. We helped the police for two years. We wasted a lot of money and got shot at a couple of times. We didn't get enough for the police to make a bust. The system said I would have to go to trial. They said they would charge someone with something, and I was the only person they had. They admitted that they knew I didn't have anything to do with it, but it was house and my land.

The guy who did it was long gone, never to come back. We went to trial. The judge asked, "How do you plead?" "Your honor I will not plead guilty to something I did not do and had no knowledge of, but I will admit I was trying to help the guy who did the crime. I had poor judgement if God wants me to do time for something I did not do it is his plan and he will provide for me" I was sentenced to 10 years. I was taken away while my mother, aunt, my finance, uncle, and many friends broke into tears. I told them goodbye and assured them everything would be okay. The prison was overcrowded so I was taken to a jail in another town. God was still in control! The prison was located in the town where my uncle lived. He got to visit me often. I stayed there for several months before an opening came in the big prison of course, I lost my home, my new truck, and a very good job! Why is this happening? It's not fair. Why am I going to prison for something that I didn't do?

After a few months I was in a big prison, the largest in the state. It was hard and lot to adjust it. My family could visit on the weekend, but it was 160 miles away. Prison isn't free. I cost a lot of money for food. Money for personal item, money to call home and lots more. Drugs are worse in prison than on the outside. Inmates swallow money and pass it later to buy drugs. Some of the guards are crooked. They also have sex with the inmates and rob your bin your keep personal staff in. A few more months passed, and I was given work release. Only an inmate were chosen. We worked in a factory. I was given quarters and lived alone. A van picked us up each morning and picked us up after work. We wore uniforms which we were charged to wear, and I also had to pay rent my "apartment". Did I tell you prison aren't free! I wasn't so bad, except being away from my family. I am adjusting, but I want somebody to know the pain I am feeling. My heart is broken, and I am not alone. My mom, brothers, sister, aunts, uncle, other family members and friends are going thru the same pain that I am feeling. It is so hard to understand why this happened. Well I always wanted a pen pal and now I have lots. Haha

Going to prison anytime is hard but going to prison you didn't do is terrible. I know I am blessed to be on work release, but I have lost so much. My dad is dead, and my mom is all alone. I have missed being with her for all this time—why? God please help me; you said you would never forsake me. I was incarcerated 30 months. As time neared for my release, I could see what God had planned for me.

I had saved enough money to buy a trucking company. April 16, 2004, I was released, and my family was there waiting for me. It was a very happy day! Thank you, God, for sending me prison. It made me a better person and made me realize how precious every minute is, so be with those you love and make every minute count. I knew God was real and talked to me when I was ten. While playing I lost my favorite pocket knife. I was so sad, a few weeks later, I was walking to a friend's house and a quiet voice came into my head. It said, "Look down".

When I did there was my knife. God told me how to find my knife. Since then he has talked to me many times and helped me survive many situations.

Tues Sept 4 2001

Hi Aunt Georgia,

First I want to tell you how much it means to me, that you are there there to help Mom through this. I also want you to read the other page, alot of that was for Both of you. That WAY I don't have to write it all Twice. I only get 4 sheets of Paper and Two Envelopes Per week. Please Tell Every one, that until I get out of here, my Two Weekly letters will be going to Debbie and you & Mom — Paul will visit and keep up with up with what is going on — Anyone who Wants to know can CAll Him & keep up with what's going on.

In your last letter you asked me about A Toyota — They are good Vehicles. As with any Import, they are Very Expensive to maintain & Repair — They are fine If you are going to trade it, before the Warranty runs out!

I never thought I would say I would be glad to get to prison — but I'll be So happy to leave here, headed to Prison, I'll be Bouncing off the WAllS! This will only be for a short time! Thanks for Everything — Give uncle Benny a Hug & Big ole Juicy Kiss — I love you Very much

Your #1 Nephew
WADE

Tues Sept 4 2001

Mom,
I hope you are O.K. - I'm glad you and
Georgia didn't make a trip to little Rock for nothing.
I hope you and Georgia aren't too Worried.
Yes this is the 2nd strictest JAil in the World -
The 1st would have to be a NAZI Concentration
camp. Don't Worry o I'm strong enough to handle
this for the short time I'll be here. IF I need
anything I have Paul. He come to see me this
AfterNoon, It made me so happy to see him I
cried, just a little. He Wanted to know If I needed
anything, money or anything - I told him they won't
let us have any money, and books have to be
Donated to the Jail - And that he just gave me
the only thing I needed - to come see me - that
Is when I lost a few tears - I don't Know If
Brad's schedule is going to let him come see
me. I tried to call Saturday, morning, but
their new Phone system didn't have 870 Area
codes programmed in. As much as it will cost,
I probably won't call but once or twice while
I'm here - But I will call as soon as they
Get the # programmed In. You got one
Wish - I quit smoking last Friday - no It
hasn't bothered me. Be Sure I let aunt
Georgia read this Also. Thank you
For All your Love & Support! "I Love you so Very"
                                    Much
Your #1 Son
    WADE.

5

Thanks for Sending Me to Prison

It can be uplifting as well as informate. Think about it. I'm convinced something good will come out of this. Raymond Robert wants your address. He said, "I really like Wade, he's a good guy."

Take care of yourself only! Don't try to help anyone, it will backfire! Save all your energy to take care of me. Yes, I think we should buy Bob's land. I can pay $20,000.00 and pay the rest later. I'll try to talk to Bob soon. Maybe Bob will help us but this place. Are you sure this is what you want?

Sat. Sept 22. 2001

At Bentonville

Good Morning Sweetheart!
To my two precious ladies
    I'm Sorry I haven't written already, but
after working all night, I sometimes sleep
too long. It is a little after 7:00 A.M.
I can Write in the morning, then it doesn't matter
if I sleep too long! Brad came to see me
yesterday morning. I was surprised, I thought
it would be Paul - he usually comes on Friday.
He must have gotten busy. I talked to Brad
for about 45 minutes, We had a good visit.
While he was here I talked to him about the
80 Acres. He is for the Idea also. He also
said that he will Co-Sign a loan for the other
20 thousand IF he has to - He said He might even
want to Buy ½ of It. I told him that wasn't
Necessary, because he can treat it like it was
his anyway. I explained to him, that I wanted
the ranch to be a retreat, that any one in our
whole family Can come use, whenever they
want. The Cabin that is already there, has 1 big
room, and 2 smaller rooms. I can take a few hundred
dollars, and 3 or 4 weekends, and turn the Cabin (Part time)
into a livable home - I plan on living there,
While I build my main House. In the beginning,
It will just be me and my dog - so I will have to go
see Debbie every 5 or 6 days! I wouldn't get anything
built if I had to deal with her!

After I finish the house, the cabin can be used by anyone in the family, any time they want to - Eventually the Cabin will be for hunting - The Women can Stay at the main House - Ha. When I am finished the Main House Will large enough to accomodate the entire Family - all at the Same place - at the Same time, at least once a year !!! It wont matter When, But It Sure is pretty on the mountain in the Winter. It snows up there more often, because of the higher elevation. Instead of having 15 Bedrooms, I am going to build one big "Bunk House" onto the Back of the House. The Ranch Will provide our Family with Hunting, Fishing, horseback riding, all the beauty & wonder of Nature and most of All Fellowship with one another. I know this Sounds like a wild dream, but It Will be easy to accomplish, and I have even figured out how to make a good living with it at the Same time. The Chicken houses that raise the eggs, for the baby Chickens that they send to the other chicken houses - I got this Idea from a man I work with, He is in his 50's. But I would rather work with him than 2 of the young guys - I will tell you his story later. To make a long story short he has 3 more months to do on a 6 month Sentence, because his young wife (½ his age) took his fine money. She thought She was paying his fines. The Night He told

(ex)

8

Me about the chicken houses, I thought about it hard for a couple hours, I Realized that If I could get him to help Me, I could have My dream, and make a very Good Living also! The next night I dropped the Idea In his lap. I didn't know what to think - He is a very Quiet, Religious Man, whose only vice is drinking Coffee, But I had to ask Any way. I had no Idea what he would think about Working with, or for, a 39 year old Man who WAS going to Prison on drug Charges! I asked him about a week ago - I was sitting at the table yesterday morning, fixing to Write you this letter, He comes over, sits down across from Me, and hands Me a piece of Paper & a pencil - He then tells me to Write down these names - His daughter & his WiFe's (NOW)(not the one who got him in trouble)(close Friend) He told me his daughter or his wife's friend will know, where they are, and how to get in touch with Him. I WAS so excited, We were Still talking, When they called Me out for Brad's Visit. He said that If we meet the requirements, that Tyson will Finance the chicken House for us for a 10 yr Plan. I can't help but feel that god brought this nice, Man into My liFe for a reason. I will talk More about this later - I have already dulled 4 of my 5 pencils, and I need to get in Bed.

I had meant to answer all you and Georgia's Questions, from your letters. I got called away. I'm going to send this letter out today, because Tomorrow may start the New week — Remember I only get 2 letters A week. I will write y'all a New one Tomorrow morning. I hope Jerry is going to be ok., I didn't mean to be insensitive, but my mind is so caught up in telling you of my plans, I almost forgot, that Ocllie told me yesterday. Afternoon on the Phone. Mom don't worry, Jerry's Tough even if they have to do a By-Pass he will come Through it alright. Mom, Please don't worry about me, Hang in there a couple more weeks, You can't miss me any more than I miss you! You know there is Nothing on this earth I would put above my love for you —

I Love you Mom —

Wade

P.S. I call me over nolser (German)
(POPS)

Georgia, I'm Sorry your personal part of this letter is So short, but I'll makeup for it tomorrow — My Pencil Is About Gone. To Answer one of your Statements Yes God Has blessed me in MANy WAYS, But none mean More to me than his giving me Two MoMs. I would Not Trade either one of you for Anything on this earth! You know he really Gave me 3 MoMs, but he has already Taken 1st of them back to heaven with him — "2 out of 3 Aint Bad" I Love YOU

WADE

① 10-20-02

Hello Mom, Georgia

I hope every thing is going Smoothly.
It was great to see the Babies last weekend.
I tried to not let the fact, that they wouldn't
let Red in, dampen my spirits. That was
very hard, considering how bad I was
wanting to see her. I wanted to hold her
close, and visit with her, not just see her!
   I hate that you all were delayed, because
of the wreck. I Just thank God, that all you had
to suffer, was a small wait. Remember when
I told you in a letter, that I was glad, that
you & Carson did'nt come In, the weekend you
were sick. It was because I had a bad feeling
about, you and Carson in a car. I am Just glad that
Red was driving, and that you all did'nt leave
a little sooner. Please be careful, in your
travels. Bob went and got Bear's heart worm
medicine, Saturday morning. He took it by to
give it to Debbie, before he came here.
Bear wouldn't Eat the tablet for him, so he
We and bought him 3 lbs. of Hamburger
Meat. I don't know what I did to ever deserve
such a great & True friend! I told him
we would get him the money, in November, when
you get back.   I Love you, Very much mom!
                              Jane

Hello Red

Thank you very much, for bringing your babies, so I could visit with them. That meant a great deal to Me, even though I didn't get to hold you. Keep your head up, and keep a strong heart, everything will work itself out, in time. Jake and Hayley looked great. I didn't know what to think, when Hayley teased Jake about his missing teeth. I know how sensitive he is. He just smiled, so I did too! Carson is something else, he wasn't satisfied with having his own soda, he had to have some of Hayley's ice cream. He proceeded to get fussy, and let us know he wasn't happy, that she wouldn't share with him. You did fill out the visitation form, before you left. I hope you did, did you think about Robbie — Even if he is never able to visit, If he ever did get a chance, I would feel bad if he wasn't approved.

They fired one of the 3 maintenance men, at work. His hours were 8:00 AM — 4:30 P.M. @ $11.25/hr. I put in my resume, even though I couldnot type it. It was worth a shot.

I miss my copy of your E-mails —

I Love you very much —

WADE

P.S. It was very hard to see you d not walk down that hall to hold you bbb —

Sunday
10-20-02

Hey JAKE

How is my little man doing? I hope
you are doing great. I hope you were
not too uncomfortable, with all those people
in the Gym. It sure was great to see you!
I will get to see you again, when I get my
week-end furlough, in December. Be careful,
when you go trick-or-treating, on Halloween.
Watch out for yourself, and for Hayley! How is
School going? I know you are doing well, in your
Studies. Be careful playing ball, I hope
you have lots of fun.
    Do you remember the time, that you almost
fell in the water head first, when me, you and
Bob went fishing. I'll never forget that! I looked
around, when you screamed, and your legs were
sticking straight up in the air, kicking, and you
were barely holding yourself out of the water.
We will go on many more fishing trips, as soon as I
get out of here. Be a good young Man, and watch
out for your Sister & little CARSON.

I Love you very much JAKE!

        Uncle WADE

Sunday
10-20-02

Hello Hayley

IT WAS Great to see you last Saturday.
Even though you are growing into a young
lady, you will always be my little girl!
I WAS very Serious, When I said, that I would
always be there for you. By always, I mean
as long as the lord lets me walk upon the Earth.
Always be true to yourself, and maintain your
self- Respect. Try not to do things, that you
cAn't be proud of. You are only human, and
all humans make mistakes. When you do make
a mistake, dont make it worse, by trying to deal
with it by yourself. As you are growing up,
you will need to let the people who love you,
help you deal with your problems, no matter
how bad they seem.
    Have you been doing your reading?
I hope so. Be a good girl, and help
look out for your brothers.

    I love you Sweet Heart ♡♡♡

            Uncle Wade

9-29-02

Hello Everyone -

Mom, you and Janaga can Both read this one letter. I will consider this as I write.

Mom, I am glad, that you did not leave last week. I am Sorry that you had a Ear Infecton, but I had a bad feeling, about you driving back. I hope you are feeling better now. If Red is having such a hard time, I think maybe you should stay a while longer. You have 2 months before I will get a furlough. I think, if for no other season, but emotional Support, that she needs you there, with her. Red, please keep a Strong heart. Keep your mind focused, on getting through this troubled period, in your life. It will make you Stronger. These hard times, will also, make your life, that you come out with, more precious. I have to confess, you have me worried. Things have never been so bad before, that you would take time to let me know what is going on. Well except when you and Robbie had that one rocky period. I know you will let me know when you are ready. Take care of Each other, and let me know how you are doing —

I love you Both, very much &&&

WADE

11-11-02

How are my 2 FAvoRite Women?
I hope you are Both doing great.
Mom, I am glad you and Amy had a good
Trip. I am relieved that you are back.
I worry about you being on the HighwAys.
I got both of your letters tonight. Yes Mom,
Every thing is fine. Nothing was ever said
about that incident. I told you not to Worry.
That WASaVery Wise writing you sent me.
Thank you George, I very much enjoyed the
E-Mails. Every thing is going smoothly at
Work. They are catering us a Thanksgiving dinner
Nov 22nd at Work - (Next Friday). We were
not off For Veterans Day. I got to WAtch
The Razorbacks Dominate South CARolina &
It WAS Great o I Almost Called Paul & Brad
After the GAME - I Will CAll them Both
soon. George I hope you are getting very
Busy, so you cAn afford to Accept my Phone CAllSo
Mom, I am glad you Will be there to help.
Give my love to Uncle Benny and Rodney.
Mom come see me when you cAn. I love
and miss you Both Very Much —

WADE

8-12-02

Hello Red

I am glad you wrote me, because
I didn't have your new Address.
I hope you have made IT BACK
Safely from your VACATION. I KNow
You Enjoyed yourself. Mom told me
that you felt like she let you down.
She had Already Given her Word.
I think/the money had some thing to
do with her not Changing her Plans.
Tell Robbie I have faith In him.
I'm proud of your Job. It IS perfect,
except for CARSON WADE. You will
find some thing that works. Robbie
will find a Job, maybe not AS Good AS
he had, but he'll come out ok. These
People here at Pine Bluff, consider
Drawings, the SAme AS Pictures. Pictures
CAN Be no larger than 5" X 7". Send
me more Info — Please Keep Working on
Getting Accepted to visit. I miss
you & I love you very much bbb

TEll Robbie, THAT
I Liked the Joke, he
Sent George and Benny

P.S. I heard the Phone # IS the SAME.
It will Be A while Before A CALL

8-12-02

Hello Hayley

I hope you had a good VACAtion.
When you write me, tell me all about
your New room. I Know you Will be
busy, but since your Grand mother can't
come stAy, until school starts, you will
have to help her alot. I WIll write
you Again soon. I think of you
Often, And wonder what you are doing!

I LOVE YOU

Very Much !!!

Uncle WADE

18

8-12-02

Hey JAKE

Did you HAVE a Good VACAtion?
I know you are Excited About A New
School yeaT. Bob has been catching
lots of Big CATfish. HANG IN there
Little Buddy. We will do lots of fishing
and camping When I get out. I miss
you Very much, I Love you as much
as If you were my own Son, not Just
my Nephew. Be CAREful — STAy SAFE

      I Love you
      Uncle WADE

P.S. Bob's Indian
NAME is
WOLF STONE!

19

10-7-02

Hello Red

    I hope everything is going well. I really enjoyed getting to see CARSON Wade Saturday. He is a Wonderful Baby. He was a big hit on the Visitation yard. He wasn't spooked a bit by all the people. He fussed pretty hard, until I gave in and let him have a taste, of my Ice Cream Sandwich. He really likes Ice cream. He thought the cherry coke was pretty good too! He likes to Gum the CAN, boy you should have seen his face the First time he got a little cherry coke. It didn't take him long, to figure out he wanted to try it again. All he was getting, was a little taste, off the rim. He lasted almost Two hours, I think he got a little tired, a lot Bored. I should be out of Prison, plc. close to his 2nd Birthday. I hope I am able to be as close to him, as I am to Haley + Jake. I am going to try - even though it is a long way off. Speaking of Haley - Do what you think is necessary, to get her to slow down + study. Mom may be a little too lenient. Give them both a Hug from me, and tell them I Love Them.

    I Love you All, Very Much

                  WADE

P.S. You might want to think about a special visit. When you come down. If you have time b

I recieved My books Last week, in 2
different Shipments. The first shipment
WAS Two books. The Century, and the
Mexican WAR book, Gone for Soldiers.
I recieved Harry Potter 4, 2 dAys LAter.
You should not have spent so much, HARRy
Potter, by Itself, Would have been great!
It was the best one yet. It WAS long,
but that was even better. I read It this
weekend. I will read, Gone for Soldiers, Next.
I hope everything goes Well, for you, over
the christmas Holidays. Please tell the
Kids, that I will see them in January.
I hope nothing happens, to keep you all
from coming — It is A Very long WAy!
Please take Good CARe of yourself!
Tell the kids, that I love them.
Thanks Again for my Books.
I love you Very much, Redd

MAy God Watch over & Keep you
all sAfe —

I love you

WADE

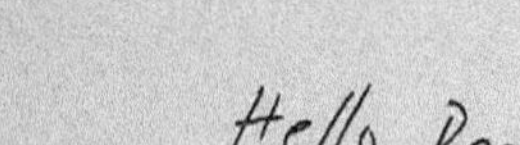

12-8-02

Hello Red

How Are you? Mom told me yesterday, during our visit, that you have been having frequent head aches. She said they were migraines. If you are having frequent migraines, you need to be checked out. It has to be something, that you are doing differently. More stress? More worry? difference in your diet? Lack of sleep? Tell Robbie I said that, maybe, you needed your tensions relieved, more often (hehe) Maybe there is something in the New house, that you are mildly Allergic to. A mild Allergic reaction, that has reached a Threshold? O.K. enough of this. You are a grown woman, and a Nurse at that.

Mom told me, that CARSON Wade is Taking his first steps. He should be getting Around good, by January. My furlough should be the 2nd, or 3rd weekend in January. I told Mom, That I wanted every one to stay together. She laughed, and reminded me that CARSON WADE, and ELIJAh, would be a handful. I told her That would be great!

22

①   1-19-03

Hello Mom, Red & Robbie

I know you made it home safely.
I talked to Georgia. I was doubly
thankful, that you were driving Mom
to Texas, Robbie. Thank you very much!
It would have been bad enough, with her
driving home, after the weekend we had,
without it snowing! It was Beautiful, though,
wasn't it. Everything is fine here. Work
went smoothly this week. My shoes feel
great. I don't know when my next furlough
will be. I will let you know as soon
as I find out. Did Anyone think
to ask Joe how close he is to Judge
Humphrey? I want To Thank you
all for Helping make this weekend possible.
It was so great to have everyone
together. I got a letter from Aunt
Lucencia, Telling me how great she thought
it was, also. Pleas Take care of Yourselvos,
And help God look out for those Wonderful Babies
of ours! Janaya, Please send your Application
In, to the visitation office.
Robbie — Don't let Joe get to you — Hang
In There
                I love you All Very much!

             WADS.

1-13-03

Hello Aunt Georgia,

I hope you weren't tired today, but after the weekend we had, you probably were. I want very much for you to understand, how much I appreciate, what you did for me this weekend. It was so wonderful, to have everyone together. This weekend would not have been possible, without a great deal of effort, and a lot of Patience, from you and uncle Benny both. I hope you didn't have to clean up a very big mess. I forgot to put up the ping-pong & pool table. I hope they won't be in the way, until I can put them up. Did Mom call you, when they got to Texas? I hope they made it without too much Trouble. It started snowing, by the time we got to Jacksonville. I had a good talk with Randy. It was short, but it was good. He really blew my mind, when he told me he would get me a Job with Pepsi, any where I wanted to go, when I get out of Louise.

That would mean I wouldn't get to
work on my place as much. It would
work great though, If I worked on my place
for 6 months or so, Before I went to work
for Him. If I only have the week-ends
to work, I will need to get the major
things out of the way first.

It took me until 11:00 PM last night,
before I wound down enough to go to sleep
I was wore out, but I lay in bed and
read a book until 11:00 PM. I woke up
about 5:50 AM - I was sore & still
a little tired. My legs were a little sore,
from playing football.

Next Month, you won't have to share
me very much — You also won't have
to worry, about every one Invading your
Home. I know we have a wonderful, close
family — But to have an Aunt that
Loves me, as much as you do, Is a special
Blessing bbb I thank God all the Time,
for Blessing me with your love!
Please Take Care of yourself, And
That Wonderful loving Man you are
Married to. & Give Him A Big Hug
From me — I Love You Both Very
much

'Darle

1   Thurs Oct. 4 2001

Good Morning Mom,
    I am glad to hear Jerry is doing O.K. Tell him I
said he needs to at least take it easy, until they
make shure everything is working properly — He doesn't
need to blow this extension God has given him,
by being hard headed. I hate that I can't call.
It would really be nice to hear your's and Georgia's
voices. I remembered Rodney's Birthday was coming up
soon, this was a couple days after Sandra's Birthday.
I'll call him tonight, I'm sure his number will go
through, since it is a 501 Area Code. When I talked
to them about getting your 510 area code to work, they
told me it would take 2 weeks, I did not think I would
be here long enough to worry about it I will have
much more time to write now, yesterday was my last
day as a Trusty, I'm glad, I was ready to quit anyway.
I will have plenty of time to Read my Books, write letters,
and hopefull Rodney will be home when I call Tonight.
It was for the Best, I was getting Tired & that was
wearing down My Self control — I almost went off
on a stupid "Bitch" Guard. That was when I decided
it was time to go back to Being a regular Inmate.
    Since Robert added the $1000, for 1 full day of
Trial, he should refund that, because we didn't go to
trial. If you call or write him another letter, remind
him that I want him to file the motion, to get the
Muzzle loader and the 22 mag num returned to you.
    I talked to Bob the other day on the phone, He
told me that he had the Timber appraised $22,000.

26

That's the figure for thinning out the Trees.
That is not Cutting All the Trees - much less the
tent Big, Pretty ones! You need to work something
out with Jim Soon, he turned down an offer
of $48,000, to Sell it to me for $40,000. I can't expect
him to Sell it to me that cheap & wait forever. But
he knows I want it for sure, and will probably hold it for
a while. There will probably be a year Before I can start
getting everything geared up to start the chicken House
Operation. I will start clearing the Sites for the house
& the road to it on my weekend furloughs from work-Release
I want everything ready to go when I get out. I should get
to a work release somewhere within the next 4 to 5 months. I
am going to save ½ of my money, until I get out. In a year's ½
I should be able to save between 5 & 10 Thousand dollars. One good
thing came from my being a trusty, besides getting to know & work with
Pops. They Pulled a man named Paul Miller out to help
strip & WAX a part of the floor. I had already been told
of him. He is well connected in the construction division
of the Arkansas department of Corrections - He is a Master
Electrician who had Already designed & wired Many
New Buildings & Additions for the Prison System.
As soon As he goes to Court & gets Sentenced, They ARE
sending him on the 1st Bus. He promised me he would be
able to reach & get me no matter where I am, He has
enough pull to have whoever he Picks on His
Electrical Crew. He said we will be building a
New Prison at Malvern - about 15 minutes South of Hot
Springs

P.S. Did ya'll check with Sheriff Bishop about a 309 "program".

Include your Phone number at your moms, and what time it would be best to call. I will be looking forward to your letter.   "Bye Connie"

Mom at least you don't have to worry about me smoking, The urge to smoke cigarettes jus isn't there any more. That also helped me decide I didn't need to be a Trusty in this hell hole any more. I was smoking cigarettes, and didn't care if I smoke them or not. It is funny How things work, a couple days after Talking to Paul Miller, God decided I didn't need to be a Trusty any more — I had gotten all I needed to out of It. They put me in the cell Block with the bunch I came up with from Pulaski County. Mom I love you very much, I hope you continue to visit Connie, she needs all the love & support she can get right now.   I'll see you soon
WADE

Hello George —
You know I really don't care what you write on, As long as you write — Before you & Mom get a wild Hair & Take off up here, make sure you call first, to make sure I'm still here, they could put us on a bus at any time, bound for Pine Bluff. You & Mom call call the diagnostic unit of the Arkansas Department of Corrections in Pine Bluff, to see If tho know when the will get me out of here! I love you WADE

He Said I can work for him until they tell me I am eligible for work release. He is not 100% sure, But he thinks we will be housed in the old Jail at Hot Springs. We will only work 5 days A week, that gives us our weekends for rest & Visitation Contact Visits - Complete with Hugs & Kisses! Jean,

I think you need to go see Shirley & talk to her. It will do you both good. Tell Connie she can write me all the letters she wants. If the letters come after they have taken us to diagnostics, in Pine Bluff, they will just send them Back. Give her the address, so she can write me, & I will send her letter with yours & Georgia's, all in the same envelope. I hope I am here no longer than 1 more week, but it might take 2 weeks to get to diagnostic - I can call sometime the same day I get those. Tell Connie it might not be as comforting to read & write letters, But since I can't hold her in my arms, it will have to do. At least until I get to where she can come visit me if she wishes to. It makes me very sad to think of her having to deal with her Mother's and She's Illnesses so close together & without much needed emotional & Physical Support. Connie if you ARe reading this, you know I will always love you, and thinking about the emotional strain you are under, hurts me deep in the depths of my Soul - I'm Sorry! I promise that I will get to you, As Soon As I CAN - Even If it CAuses problems with my current girlfriend! If you WANT me to CALL you when I get to Pine Bluff,

Pg. 2   Tuesday, Oct 9 2001

Good Morning Mother,
    I have had a very good Morning, as far as a
Morning can go in Jail. It started about 2:00
when the deputy was calling people out, for the
bus ride to the Pen. They called our room, but
it was my cell mate's name. A few minutes
later, I heard the door mechanism open, I got excited
because I thought I was next. It was only my
cell mate coming back, I felt so sorry for him,
they got his name mixed up. That had to be very
disappointing. He is one of the 10 or 12 people left
that came up with me from Pulaski. They usually
take 15 or 20 people out on a Pen run, this morning
they only took 7. Hopefully Friday Morning will
be my day to go, & if not, it will for sure be
next week. After all that excitement, it was hard
to get back to sleep. Wake-up for breakfast
comes about 5:00 - 5:30. After breakfast, we clean
our cells. I was in church when Brad got
                                            over
there for my Visitation. Whether his knee was
really broken or not, because he is getting around
fine, and he said the pain is gone. If he believes
God healed his knee, who are we to say he didn't.
All that matters to me is that his knee is healed.
I started this letter about 10:30 AM, dinner will
be here around 11:00 AM, I got to talk to Georgia
Saturday afternoon at Rodney's, I put off her
Birthday Call until then so maybe she would be
                                        there,

Monday, 24 Sept 2001

Good Morning Sweetheart

I was going to write you yesterday morning, but there was a mix up in the Kitchen. It took us till about 9:00 am to finish feeding Breakfast. I'm glad it worked the letter Saturday, because Sunday Starts a new week. I wouldn't have gotten any letters mailed last week, if I hadn't mailed it. I hope everything is going Smoothly with Jerry's heart. I will call Debbie Tuesday afternoon, she will fill me in!

I will now answer your Questions:

As a Trusty my extra privileges are; ① My Mattress is Twice as Thick, ② Our cell doors don't have locks, Just the Door that goes outside the cell block, ③ a little more food at each meal - Since we work from 11pm till 7AM We get to eat at about 11 PM - So If I want to get up for Dinner (I usually Sleep) I can eat 4 meals a day, ④ access to an electric Razor + Clippers, ⑤ We get to Smoke, ⑥ Since we work in the laundry room, we get clean clothes every day, and finally, they are not as strict on us in general. for example, My medical slip for my Ibuprofen from the Nurse, ran out last week, but very few of the Deputies will Say no If a Trusty ask for Some Ibuprofen.

Please tell Connie that I am very Sorry, that I could not be with her during this very emotional time. Tell her that As Soon as I get to prison, I will write her. You will have to get her address for me!

Yes I do get to go outside some, Sweeping Sidewalks carrying out Trash, or standing outside talking to Deputy McVey - We have gotten to be pretty good friends.

I told him I wished I would have met him under different circumstances, and he said it made him no difference, for me to look him up when I got out of prison. He is going to come down & go Bear Hunting. I told him he could drive to the Ranch in about 1 hour and 45 minutes — he laughed & said he can make it in 1 hour — then we walked outside & he showed me his Dodge 4 wheel drive. ● No the Bentonville preacher has not came to visit me. No, I can't have Pictures, but they did let me keep the ones that Taylor & McKenna drew for me — I should only be here 1 more week maybe 2. Here is what we do:

① 7pm — all Six of us go to the laundry room — 4 of us work on the laundry, and 2 of us work on the floors. Mrs. Overholser is one of our 2 floor buffers. We work for a couple hours, and go take a smoke break. We work for a couple more hrs, eat supper & then take another smoke break, what happens next depends on which deputy is the Rover. The Rover runs the Cleaning crew. Beside washing clothes, & buffing the floors, we have to clean the whole Jail (except the cell blocks — they have to clean them themselves.) Then we take another smoke break, The last thing we do is feed all the Inmates and pick up all the trays and take them back to the Kitchen. If nothing happens during breakfast we usually get done from 7-7:30.

I am proud you are walking, It will keep you healthy, look what It did for Pa Pa! You have got to stay healthy & stay on this Earth with me for a very long time. God can do without you for a while longer! I Hope — I don't Even want to think about what I will do If any thing happens to you! I get plenty of Exercise, there is no telling how much I walk during the course of A 12 hr Night. My legs were sore for the First Few days. That is not a bad choice for a title for a book. Especially since being in Jail has shown me how many Young boys & Girls need Guidance — It is so sad — It makes me want to start some kind of program to help as many as I CAN. First things First, I have to Get our Ranch up and running, and build my house — I am 100% Sure I want us to buy Bob's 50 Acres. Tell Jerry yall have to come visit every other weekend, or you will have to Find another Boyfriend, HA — tell him see what he says! Tell Paul he can stay with me if he CAN get his daddy to buy us a full Size Back toe! If Jerry doesn't get him on an exersize program along with a healthy diet he is going to out live Paul! — Don't worry about me smoking, It wasn't a problem before so it won't be a problem once I get To Prison — I hope they call my number Soon — TAKE CARE of yourSelf — I love you very much
WADE

Hello George,

I am really glad you write me letters too.
Tell Momma I said to stop making *you write* all your letters
on little bitty pieces of paper! (HA) I wish I could
see y'all too, but hopefully I wont be here, but I maybe
2 more weeks. Then they will send me to diagnostics,
I will be there 7 to 10 days. They *will* check me out from head
to Toe, that is why it will take so long. They will then send
me to a prison, I wont know which one until I get there (diagnostic)
Once I get to prison, every weekend we can have contact
visits — we can hug & kiss — yeah
I need you or mom to ask sheriff Bishop if
Newport has a "309" program, It is like a work release
program, where I work for the county sheriff. If they do, find
out all the details. Don't worry about how the walls look,
as long as you like it, it will be ok. Uncle Benny
wont care as long as you are happy with it! Have
Robby to find you an American made sport utility vehicle.
If you get a program car, they usually have from 10-20 K
miles - still in warranty and will save you thousands of
dollars — Chevrolet has a new one - inbetween a
Tahoe and a Blazer - you might want to check it out!
Tell Rodney that once I get to prison and can have pictures
I want one of his truck - Give uncle Benny a big
hug for me — You have always been very special
to me. Tell uncle Benny that he has 2 years to get
his life scaled down to where he doesn't work all the
time. Tell him y'all are going to have to split your

Friday, November 2 2001

Hello Mom,

It's Friday morning, and they haven't called for me. I will have to spend another week-end here. The next bus doesn't run, until Monday or Tuesday. Today marks my 9th week here. November 9th will mark 3 months, since I have been sentenced. That will leave 24 to 27 months, until my parole Date. I'm sure will go by fast enough, If I can just get the hell out of here!

I guess you decided not to get Dot's land. That's fine, I'll find some land, somewhere close to Batesville. I just thought it would have been nice to be close to Brad and Janaga Both. We will be hard pressed to find 80 acres for 18 thousand dollars (40 for the land — 22 for the timber) One thing I do know, is that I don't want anything to do with any of the McNutt land! Period!

I guess you are not going to help out, by getting her some Dog food. If you were going to, you missed a damn good chance, when she had her clad with her at Tuckerman. It is not like I am asking you to pay her bills. It doesn't take But $15.00 a month to feed MY Dog!

I love you

WADE

Hello Georgia,

I wish my letter would be coming to you from Pine Bluff, I'll at last be here a few more days — The next load will be Monday or Tuesday Morning —

I hope Rodney and uncle Benny got alot accomplished on his truck. I am not going to call again at Rodney's — The next time you hear my voice, will be when I call you from Pine Bluff That way I'll be in a better mood! Tell Mom not to stress over Bob's land, I'll find some when I get out of Work Release in 2 yrs. I'm going to call him today and tell him to sell it to the Man who offered him 48 thousand —

Thanks for everything, I hope to be calling you early next week — Give cuddle Benny a hug for me —

Lotsa Love

WADE

                                        Monday, Sept 10, 2001

Mom & Georgia — Greetings from
your #1 Son and Nephew! It's Monday,
time for my 2 weekly letters — To y'all and to Debbie.
Being in a situation like this, you realize what
is important, in life. To me, enjoying the outdoors,
spending time with my family & friends, and my dog —
It really make a person feel loved, when members
of his family expend so much time & effort,
just to spend a few precious minutes together.
I hope you got your letter from last week ok.
You can't ever tell around here. There's no Erasers sorry
Tuesday, Paul came to see me, to start my
weekly visits. I thought Paul would be my
only visitor, because of Brads work schedule,
boy was I surprised! Wednesday morning
they tell me I have a visit, I'm thinking it's Paul
again, Boy was I surprised, to find that
Debbie had gotten her Dad to drive her
all the way up here for a 30 minute visit.
After we eat our noon meal, they let us
take a nap — Wednesday afternoon, during my
nap, I get a call, saying I have another visit.
I walk to the visitation room, and there is
No-one there. I was so surprised to see
Brad and his whole family walk in. The
little shit took off work and brought his
whole crew with him! Elijah is getting so Big!
I talked to each of the kids, then Brad, I

Ginger, then I was talking to Brad again, when we all noticed that Elijah was trying his best to get through the glass. He got mad, when he could not get through, and beat on it with his little hand. That touched me so deeply that I couldn't help but cry! Brad came to see me again Thursday morning. He came a little after 8:00 am. We got to visit almost an hour — He got them to move him to a clinic, close by, just for that day. Paul came by Friday afternoon after work, around 3:00 pm. We got to visit until almost 4.00 pm. When they aren't busy — early & late — you get longer visits. Paul also talked to the captain, who told him, to tell me, to fill out a trusty application. I got an application from the sergeant, fill it out, and turn it in. We have mail call before lock-down, at 8:00, I get a letter from Bob. He had already sent it once & had the wrong address. I get a call Saturday, after supper, to go to booking — I'm thinking it is over my trusty application. I walk in there, and boy am I surprised to see Red & the whole family. It was after hours, plus on Saturday — & it was because they came from out of state — we still only got 30 min. When they got here they got mad — Red & Robbie still had AR. drivers license. They thought they had lied to them.

over on back — sorry but they only give
us 2 envelopes & 4 sheets of paper

38

We had a good visit — I got to see my
babies — almost all of them. Bob & Landon
are trying to work his schedule out to where they
can come up — but that will have to wait —
He better stay his ass in school! I know
It is really bothering yall not being able to
get away & come up, but that OK. Just hold
on for a few more weeks, and we'll get
visits where I can give Yall Big Hugs &
Kisses ———— I can't wait —
I love you both more than you will ever
understand. I hope you know how much
your love and support means to me! Now
Give each other a Hug — Don't Forget uncle
Benny — That will have to hold you over
until you can have the real thing —
                    I love you Both Very Very much—

                              Wade

P.S. Brad is very excited

about the 80 acres of Bob's,
He is wanting to go this year & Hunt — So is Taylor

I told Bob he said it would be O.K. —
I wish you would talk to him (Bob) He said
He had people trying to Buy it — but I already
knew that — I def. want it if we can work
it out —

Benny Payne

From:	<JanagaTrotter@aol.com>
To:	<Lottie@crosscountybank.com>; <trottermania@yahoo.com>; <JTRNet30@hotmail.com>; <jsosebee@bankersbank.com>; <trotter@wpoin.com>; <TWONEWMAN@aol.com>; <cheerchick_claire@hotmail.com>; <kellyeramsey@hotmail.com>; <Celestem@imajeamericas.com>; <AMStrickerrn@hotmail.com>; <CaraKay@ipa.net>; <CNMoery@yahoo.com>; <cooper@wpoin.com>; <Shauna@ipa.net>; <Adstfml5@hotmail.com>; <autumlewis@hotmail.com>; <pch4@mindspring.com>; <VJB@cei.net>; <Whdjgriffin@cs.com>; <hcooper@astate.edu>; <dwolvert@cswnet.com>; <ptyner@cox-internet.com>; <bgkeller@ipa.net>; <Lillybsmith@aol.com>; <Krshepherd@aol.com>; <SAFARIGUY3588@gateway.net>; <ilbird@rcn.com>; <JoCrew@vci.net>; <molgranny@aol.com>; <briggs@fastdata.net>; <james.kautt@student.uni-tuebingen.de>; <fayek@dellepro.com>; <fourts84@alltel.net>; <Cassymarfar@hotmail.com>; <lmshepherd@ualr.edu>; <info@bentonville-church-of-christ.org>; <CLBOAT2716@aol.com>; <DBurne6573@aol.com>; <Melnee5091@aol.com>; <Chavezdsc@aol.com>; <angie422@mail.com>; <BRDpath@aol.com>; <GRAEBER@gateway.net>; <wilma_lopez@prodigy.net>; <insman@ipa.net>; <JavierJ651@aol.com>; <kraps1@juno.com>; <robjmartin@hotmail.com>; <mca.mccorkle@worldnet.att.net>; <sandra7509@webtv.net>; <RNORRIS71@aol.com>; <bpayne@ipa.net>; <MOSWALT@percon.com>; <simmons4@ipa.net>; <WASpurlock@juno.com>; <DLTapp@earthlink.net>; <Cartram2@aol.com>; <Marglen@tcac.net>
Sent:	Tuesday, September 11, 2001 11:33 AM
Subject:	Attack on America

I'm pretty sure everyone is in shock as much as my family is at this moment.
My children and I were watching the news when we saw the 1st building on
fire. We were all watching when the 2nd plane attacked. Jake, my 6 yo son,
said exactly what I was thinking....Is this real, Mom? It was one of my worst
nightmares. Hayley, my 9 yo daughter, said Mom, it's like watching the
scariest movie ever. Out of the mouths of babes. Please pray for all the
families of the lost ones, the rescue workers, and the United States. We were
in the car on the way to school, when I suggested that we pray for what has
happened. Hayley asked if she could say it. I listened with tears in my eyes
as she said, " Dear God, Please be with the people in those 2 buildings, with
the people on the planes, and please help the United States from being in a
war. Amen" I was so proud. She actually understood what was happening. How
scared she must be. How scared we all are. Who would have thought this would
ever happen to us. I'm not sure who all will be affected by this, not sure if
any family or friends were in this catastrophe. Our prayers are with
everyone. Not just the ones affected now, but what will happen to the United
States. Pray for our leaders, that they will know what to do. I personally
have been on my knees several times this morning, praying for help from God.
He is the one we must rely on. Be thankful we have him. God Bless everyone.
Sorry if this rambled, but I know I'm still in shock. I occasionally think
I'm dreaming, but then I watch the news and just cannot believe this has
happened. PLEASE PRAY!
Love everyone and God Bless and have mercy,
Janaga Trotter

Hello Mom,

I love you & I hope you are doing well. I know its hard to stay positive, when so many terrible things are happening around you. The thing that has been heaviest on my mind, is uncle Butch. Who is going to help them take care of the horses. I don't know if it is possible, but if Wade Horsey and his mom can convince sheriff Bishop to pull me out on a "309" Program — I would be tickled to death to help them. Even if I have a regular job to do around the jail, Maybe sheriff Bishop will let me go out there part of the Day thru the Week, & on weekends The "309" program is where a county sheriff makes an arrangement, with the Arkansas Department of Corrections, for an inmate to be Transfered to his county Jail to Work for his County. It resembles a Work-Release program — Any County sheriff can do it if he wants to Take responsibility for the prisoner. 2 months after I get to prison, I am eligible for Work Release, or the "309" program. The Work system in prison is Based on what "CLASS" you have obtained. AS soon as I got there, I will be a "class 2". I have a Mandatory 60 days labor at the prison, once I have completed my 60 days, I will move up to a "class 1". You have to be a "class 1" to leave the prison grounds without a guard escorting you — "Work release" or "309" either one has to be a "class 1" — I will be Working for at least My 60

Hello Georgia –
I hope Mom is not Too Jealous about
you getting to talk to me Twice – you don't
understand how good it makes my heart feel,
to be able to talk to ya'll. Tell uncle Benny
It's ok that he was Eating, I'll talk to
Him once I get to diagnostics, tomorrow.
I hope very much that I am on that Bus
in the morning – Don't worry, as soon as
I get there, when ever it is, The 1st call
I make will be to you! I want you & Mom
To have uncle Benny Take a Picture of ya'll
in front of your Paint Work when you are
finished, Tell Mom that since it is easy to do,
and it is free, she could E-mail Janaga
more than once a week – I hope you &
Mom are Taking advantage of this nice
weather for your Walks –
Don't Worry, Rodney is content with his life,
& when he gets ready to Dive off into the
Deep end – you can Bet the Farm that
He will Be sure it is the right woman
for him & It will be a woman that He
cant Live without & STAY Strong Hearted
& STAY Positive –
                        I love y'Gu very
                           much –
P.S. Give uncle Benny
a Hug & Kiss for   WADE
P.S. I Called him – – 01 – –

"Normally your 1st 60 days are done on a "Hoe Squad" - that is where a group of Inmates are chained together swinging a hoe that weighs about 8 pounds. If a person is over 40 yrs. old he doesn't go on the "Hoe Squad". If it is 40° or colder the "Hoe Squad" Stay inside! Even if I did have to go - this is the best time of year. I will do Electrical work at Malvern for 3 or 4 months - or until they come get me for work Release! I talked to Carl Miller, who will be my supervisor at Malvern just 3 days ago - I shouldn't be at Pine Bluff but a couple Weeks before he is able to pull me - at the most a month - I may be at Diagnostic for a couple weeks - I have to get out of there before I can go any where else. Well, there are 5 people left of the 27 that came in with me, 4 people left Monday morning, one of them my room mate - It made me think they had come for me - More than likely there will be another load out in the morning - I hope I am on It!!! I know you have alot to do, but please help Connie all you can, and please call uncle Butch and that wonderful Wife he has - tell him I'm praying for him and If they can swing it - I will gladly put off going to work release to Help them out! I Love you sweetheart - Hang in there we are on the down Hill Side Now ——

P.S. I called Brad Sunday - He was emotional   WAOS

Nov. 27th, 2001

Hello Sweetheart,

I hope you got ahold of Krissy. I hope you were Able to impress upon her the importance of her taking CARE of this. She needs to know that, if I have to, I will take Her to court, and have Landon to testify against Her, if She pushes me to that point. Please keep these originals at your store, and make copies. I'm Sorry to have to put you in this position. If I hadn't trusted her to take care of this, we wouldn't be in this position. I don't know how yet, but I will make all this up to you, when I get out of this mess I have gotten myself into. The next time you write me, would you please include Bobby & Leucenia's Phone number - never mind - I'll get them to give it to me when I write them. I feel Bad - I have only written them 1 time - while I WAS in Pulaski County - I Love You - Gotta Go - Thank's for Everything

WADE

(3) Have a SAFE & HAPPY New Year
                    I Love You!

Hello George,

I got your letter today, thank you
very much for adding Red's E-mail —
It was very nice to be able to talk
to ya'll on the Speaker Phone. — It WAS
almost like being there., I Know you
will be kind a busy this week, too,
but I was hoping you could slip away
Saturday, Jan, 5, & if not, surely you
can make it by the 19th, I know you
probably can't come the 5th — Maybe not even
the 19th, but I had to let you know any way
I'll understand if you can't come — It's o.k.
After the 19th, I believe I can start getting
visits every week-end — Since I was unassigned
for the 1st week, it might be the 26th before I
Get to Class E. When you talk to Rodney
Again, tell him I am going to get me a Harley,
to rebuild, Then I will have one to ride with
him & Bobby ———— I know he told me that
he would save that Honda for me in his shed —
Tell him that I hope he doesn't move before
I get out — I have got that motorcycle traded
for a Truck — (Either a '74 Wrecker, or a '88 1 TON
                                                    dually)
P.S. Don't forget to give   I Love You
uncle Benny His   Wade
          Nuts!

Hello George —

HAVE you WALKed this week?

I hope you and uncle Benny are doing well. Is his Mother any Better? Please tell her that I wish her a speedy recovery. This month has gone by pretty fast! I hope July goes by quickly, Also. By August, I should know something about Work-Release. Remember my friend, that was going to get us the "309" slots, at Dumas. He is leaving soon, for "309" at stone county. He needed something Positive, because his dad died last saturday night, or early Sunday morning. Heck of a fathers Day, Huh. He got an emergency furlough, for a few hours saturday. After his visit saturday afternoon, it was like his dad was waiting for his visit; before he Passed on! They Also let him out to go to the funeral Tuesday. As I sat outside the Pump house, watching the thunderstorm approach, I started counting my blessings! I have been blessed with quite a few lately. As A Result, of all the prayers, on my Behalf. ① I missed the time of year, for chopping grass with those Big Hoes, + All I had to do was Pick up Pecans. ② I got an easy Job Inside, as an electrician ③ Krissy finally took CARE of my Detainer. I got a good Job outside, At the Med unit. Now I have this better Job at the Pump House. ④ Soon I will be going to Work Release. Bye Now, Love WADE

"Keep WAlking"

I hope to see you soon —

I Love you Very Much &&& — Give uncle Benny a Hug for me &

46

Thursday 6-13-02

Hello George

Have you recuperated from your trip?
I got your letter yesterday, but I already
knew where you had gone. I called Rodney
Monday night. I bet the weather is
nicer up there — loss Humidity. The
Native American Center In Indianapolis Indiana,
is where the Two Feathers clan, operates out
of. Yes, that IS the clan that I will
get adopted into, when I am free once again.
Mine and Bob's friend, Peppe, Just got adopted,
LAST week. He had to go, to the Big Piney
Reservation, In South Dakota, for the Adoption
ceremony. They have started getting the
Dance grounds ready for the Annual Sun
Dance. It will start next week. It last
About a week. They hold theirs in Southern Illinois.
Another group will hold one A week later IN the
Southern Indiana. — got side tracked didn't I.
I Love you very Much — I hope to See you Soon
How is your Back? Did It hold up ok, on
your trip, I hope So — ARE you still Walking?
I hope God will watch over, and keep you
Both Safe on your Journey's.
                    I Love you Both Very Much

WADE

47

Sunday May 19, 2002

Hello George

I am very sorry, that I didn't call you
Friday. I didn't realize, that you look forward
to our friday talks, as much as I do. I just
thought, that it would save you a little money.
I'm sorry, it won't happen again — I'll call
you on friday afternoon — 3:30 - 4:30 — Every
friday. I Enjoyed my visit Saturday.
It was good to see Blad & Mom, but seeing
McKenna & Taylor really recharged my soul!
Did mom tell you, what McKenna said, while
waiting for me to get out there? She
noticed every one wearing white outfits,
and she asked mom, "Mimi, are all those
guys Painters?" When mom told me that
I almost fell out of my chair laughing.
It was really good, to get to see Rodney last
Saturday — It had been since last August.
    I started a different Job Friday — It is
real easy — as long as nothing tears up!
I watch over the large pumps, that are responsible
for pumping the sewage, from the whole Prison, to
the treatment Plant. I check them about once, or
twice an hour — I am at work now!
I have Alot of time to Read & write letters.
I am going to try & write everyone today & tomorrow!
            I Love you — Wade

Give uncle Benny A Big Hug!

48

Sun 6-2-02

Hello George

I hope everything is going smoothly for
Mrs Payne. It was good to hear you in
good spirits Friday, in spite of being
by yourself. I didn't call Rodney Friday.
I'll call him this evening, that will give
him time to be home (In case he came to Newport.)
I had to switch Ink Pens - The blue one
was running out of Ink - (very aggravating.)
I was off yesterday, and Wednesday, this
week - I'll only get one day off Next week.
I had a good visit with Debbie. Her Mom,
and a friend of hers, brought Debbie to visit.
They dropped her off, and then went shopping
in Pine Bluff, until they picked her up at 3:00 PM
We had a good Visit, and she was tickled,
because she had me all to herself.
After our visit, I tested out my Left
Shoulder, by playing hand ball. It was
the first real sweaty work out I have
had, since I hurt it 6 weeks ago. (Rotator Cuff
It is still sore If I rotate my Arm, (muscle)
But It didn't Hamper my playing much. The
extra 25 pounds did! HA - I still did alright
for A fat Boy! I plan on playing, After
work today, to work out my soreness from yesterday
I'll call you Friday - I love you very much!
Dad's

P.S. Tell Mrs Payne that I send My Good Wishes & Prayers. Give uncle Penny A Hug

①   Tuesday 2-5-02

Hello

    I hope by the time this Letter reaches ya'll, that my Mother has made it home safely. I hope everything goes well, and I get to see ya'll Saturday. I Know you will leave as soon as you can, that will not make the waiting any easier, I hope you can get here soon enough, so we can have a table. I Won't CARE if we have to sit in the floor, as long as I get to see you —

    One thing you might want to consider, 4 people can come. It does'nt matter who is coming, I want you to call the visitation office, and make sure there will be no problems, at the gate. Debbie and her Mother came Saturday, and Mrs. Patsy had to sit in the Truck. I think it was because her drivers license said Patsy Aelring — not Patsy McWhitt. I had to cut my visit real short — I could not leave her sitting in the Truck. I thought you might want to call Lucenia, or Amy. If he has time, I would love to see Rachey. If Lauren comes, she will count as a person. Please call the visitation office, I have waited so long to see ya'll, I don't want Anything to ruin this visit. Your map is on the other page. Be very careful - I love you!

    See you ~~Saturday~~

    Uncle

P.S. I am almost out of coffee.

(2)

AS you travel down I-30 south—
When you pass the Roosevelt Road Exit,
Be prepared to Exit left. (Get in the left lane)
AS you exit left, <u>Be CAReful</u> <u>not</u> to
take the Airport Exit, keep going toward
Pine Bluff—

Once you ARE on I-65 headed TOWARD Pine
Bluff— STAY on that SAME Road
until you see A Big Brick sign that
SAys Cummins Prison— I will Be on your left
AS you head out PAST Pine Bluff, you will notice
The Road changes to a 2 lane, After about
30 minutes—(on a Bus?)—YOU Will NOT Be Able
to miss the little town of Grady, AR. The
Turn off is a short WAY PAST Grady. The 1st
Prison will be VARNer, on your right—keep going PAST
VARNer—YOU CANT miss It—Be CAReful

Monday Dec 3, 2001

Hello Mom.

I hope you had a good Week-end.
Sunday was great, We got to goo out on
the yard for 2 hours. The weather WAS
pretty. Me and 2 of my close friends walked
between 2 & 3 miles. One time around the
yard is between 1/4 + 1/2 a mile. We would
walk a lap & I would go over & do some
push - ups - I must have done some good,
My shoulders + CALVES are sore. I go to
school All day on Monday, and 1/2 day on
Thursday. It is G.E.D. School, I will have
to go until they get my records from Newport
High School. I thought about going to
Vo-Tech school it last a year. They won't
pay me while I am going, and I won't get
a 48 hour furlough once a month, like I
will in Work-release. They don't allow
college courses - that is in Federal Prison.
I guess I will get my first taste of working
tomorrow, It will be above 42° F and not
raining. Today they picked Broccoli, and Carrots.
I have 45 more days on Hoe Squad, then
I will go up for my classification. I will
get my class 1, along with a decent Job, and
START working on getting to a Work-Release.

I should be able to get the work release I WANT, in 1-2 months. They have them in, Pine Bluff, Benton, Blytheville, Texarkana, and Springdale. I am going to put in for Pine Bluff #1, and Benton as my #2 choice. I should only need you to send me money, for 4 more months. As for as your budget goes, I'll leave that up to you. I would like to have at least $25.00 per week, but if you can spare it, send up to 50. The Maximum I can spend per week is $55.00. If things get tight, I'll make out with whatever I have to. I am just grateful that you are sending me any. We go the the store on Tuesdays & Thursday, so I will be spending the last of my money Tomorrow. Please send me some, as soon as you can, so I can go to the store next Tuesday. AS long AS it gets here this week-end, that will be soon enough. Get with Georgia, She knows how to send it the proper wAy. Having you and Georgia looking out for me, while I am in here, means more to me than you may be able to comprehend! I almost cried when I got the picture of my Babies Today — They grow so fast. Thanks for the picture. I love you very much Mom —
WADE

pg 3

Hello George,

I hope you had a wonderful week-end the weather was so pretty, you had no excuse for you & Mom not to WALK. Thank you very much for calling Kirsty. I wish you would remind Mom to stay in touch with Landon, as much as possible. I wish she would check, in a week or so, & make sure she has filled out & turned in those Child Support papers.

I know I will have to do without seeing you for a while, but I'm O.K. with that. This means that your business is doing well, and it would be very selfish & stupid of me, to want you to leave uncle Benny, at the busiest time of the year. Don't worry, just keep writing me those wonderful letters, yes to me they are all wonderful — even the very short ones! I will make it through this just fine. It helps, to have a good support group! It was hard not to call this weekend, I will call Saturday between 12:00 & 1:00 pm on Saturday. Talk to mom about a time I can call & talk to her — Thanks for Everything. I will Never forget all this! I love you, WADE

Tuesday 26ᵗʰ

Hello George

I hope you are having a wonderful day.
I want you to know how special you are
to me. It is perfectly normal for a mother to
give her own son unconditional love, even
if he doesn't always deserve it, but for
someone else to show that kind of love & support,
is very special. Hopefully Krissy will take
care of that detainer, and I can get to the
Benton Work-Release Center. It will be less
of a hardship to visit me there, I also
will get 48 HRS furloughs after 60 or 90 days.
Have you talked to Amy or Lucenia? You
said something, about them wanting to visit. I
will write them both today. I will wait until
Friday Afternoon to call, Incase I might
get to catch mom or Janusa — I will call
Paul & Brad Sometime this week. I hope
everything is well with Rodney & uncle Benny.
Give them my love & The weather will be
pretty soon, and you & mom can start walking
Again — Please TAKE CARE of yourself
I love you very much

WADE

I forgot
you will
Be AT
Rodney's

Tuesday 26th

Hello Mom

I hope you are feeling better. It made me very happy, to see you and Georgia Saturday. I had my doubts, as to whether you would make it on time, or not. I hope to see you again soon. I hope that Krissy does like she said, and takes care of that detainer. I got 10 Envelopes and a new writing pad yesterday. I was proud of that, so I could write every one, but I was equally proud to get my cushion Insoles, for my Boots. There was no work today. There was a prison wide shake down. They did everything but strip search us. Times like this make me glad I am not breaking any rules! I will get to visit with my buddy, Kenny, tonight at church. The 1st thing he'll do is worry me about that detainer, but that just shows he cares! I have 7 dollars left out of the $50 Georgia sent, send me what you can spare. Tell Janaga I'll write her, and it should be waiting on her, when she gets home next week! Thanks for everything, I love you very much!

WADE

Hello George,

Thank you for Calling Debbie.
You knew I would be wondering, If
it had been taken care of. When I
talked to Debbie Sunday, She still wasn't
feeling well, so I didn't get all the facts.
It is taking All my self control not to
waste a phone call. I can wait until I
talk to you Thursday - Friday IF I can
wait that long - If Krissy took care
of the letter to the child support office,
I need you to follow up on it. Please
call the child support people to confirm,
that they recieved the letter. Then
let them know we would appreciate them
letting the sherriff's office know ASAP!
Then let the sherriffs office know how much
we would appreciate them passing this
Information on to Cummins ASAP.
I Am eligible for work-Release as soon as
the detainer is lifted. I will be eligible
for a "309" slot on May 19th. We
can discuss all our options Saturday,
I Hope - Give uncle Benny A Hug, for me.
I love you very much

WADE

Hello Mom

I talked to Georgia Friday, and was very happy to hear, that you were quickly returning to your old self. That means you're feeling much better!! I would have liked to talk to you Friday, but I realize, that you had a lot going this week-end. I hope everything went well, with Jerry's procedure. Debbie was sick enough, that she had to spend 2 days at her Mom's. Bob's ornery ass hasn't been taking his heart medicine, and almost had to go to the hospital. Maybe all four can come this week-end. I called Brad's this week-end, and they have all been sick, but were better now. Have you talked to them lately? He was worried about the child support deal. From what Debbie tells me, It has been taken care of, I hope so. Take care of yourself — don't overdo it Just because you feel better! I hope to see you this week-end —

I LOVE YOU VERY MUCH!

WADE

What's up JAKE?
Not much Here, Just reading and
Enjoying This good Weather. It
Won't be long - a few days to a week - until
It will be Hot + Humid! It will stay
That way, until sometime in September!
By the Time It cools off - In October,
I will only like a Short while, a few months,
until I get out for good. Then we can make
up for Lost time. We will go fishing
and camping, and as Soon As I get some
horses, you can come + go riding Anytime
your mom will Let youd. I know you
are only my Nephew, but in my heart,
I love you as much as If youd were my
own Son. I hope as you get older, that
We can still be buddies, and do lots of
fun things Together. Take CARE of Yourself
and Stay SAFE.
I love you very Much, JAKE.
You are a Big 8 yrs old now - And I am
very Proud of youd

P.S.
I hope you enjoy
your New GAME!

uncle
WADE

I Talked To uncle Benny Awhile
AGO, He said, That you and Georgia
were SHOPPing in Jonesboro. IT WAS
a beautiful dAy to get out. He told
Me to CAll BAck. I will get You to
look up Connie's Address at the liquor
STORE. I wish you would CAll SHiRley
Tomlinson BAck, And Get Her Address
or LiSH's AT Home, Wherever SHirley
ThinkS I Should Write.

Please remember to See About Getting
My Driver> license ReinstAted and
Renewed.

I Hope to Get to TAlk To All of you
In a few Hours —

I love you All vERY Much

WADE

① 3-9-03

Hello Mom

I hope you enjoyed your STAY With
DAWN, and her New BABY. Georgia
Said that you stayed a couple of days.
How WAS uncle Russ. I got the
letter that you wrote Wednesday, Yesterday.
They had Sent it to a Barracks. —
How old IS Tyler? - (— months)
WAS Charlotte still there?
   I really enjoyed the article.
I'm glad that Janaga and the Kids
made it safely. I was supposed to call
BACK last night, after you got to Georgia &
Benny's, I am sorry, But I got into a Good
Book, and It slipped my mind. We have
been blessed, with some beautiful weather.
I hope ya'll have TAken advantage of It!
How long ARE you going to Be At Georgia's
I hope, at least long enough to get This
Letter. ARE you going to Be Spending
a lot of Time at Jerry's? If you ARE,
I am going to need the Address.

Hello Everyone!

I hope you are all doing well.
Did you enjoy your Trip? I Think
so.

I hope This reaches you Before
Sunday, Jan. 29. I will call sunday
Evening, around 8:00 Pm. If you
aren't home, I'll Try Again at 9:00 Pm.

Mom, How did you get to Texas?
Did you drive The Explorer? When
ARE you coming BACK TO ARKANSAS?

IT reached 80°F Today at Little Rock.
I guess spring is here. If This weather
remains spring-like, The Fish Should be
real active by April 4th. I have To
let Landon Know When, So he can
get off Work. I Am Supposed to let
Paul Know, Also. I am doing Fine.

Well It is Almost 9:00 Pm — My Bed time.
I'll TALK To Everyone SundAy — I Love
And Miss you All Very Much bbb

HAVE A HAPPY Birth day, Red

P.S.
I'll send
The Book Title
list LATER —

Wade.

62

Hello Everyone!

I hope Everyone is Doing great.
I Also Hope My HAppy Birthday Wishes,
Make It on Thursday, February 6th!
I hope you Enjoy your Birthday
Very Much. I cAlled Georgia, FridAy
Afternoon, and She told me thaT Robbie
took the Finance Job — I think thAT
WAS A Wise decision. Robbie, It Will
be good to get More experience in
Finance — thAt Is Norprally A
Very High PAying Position. Remember
PATRick PAT, at BAlE — HE Averaged $13,000
A Month, for a few Months — I think
It will Be good, Even If you don't
get A Demo. Now You & Joe can Be
Friends & noT HAve to Work together.
I Am glAD The Shuffle didn't
Crash on your House & Debris fell
pretty close to ya'll, Though Didn't It?
I Won't Bc reading Much, or Writing
Much, Till This Weekend. I am
Working from 5:00 Am till 4:30 PM, on
Wednesday & Thursday / I'll have
to get Up About 3:30 Am.

③

THAT'S OK, I'll GET 6 HRS of
OverTime.

Bob Came SATurdAy, for a while.
We had a Good UiSiT. He talked to
Duke the other DAy. Duke told Bob,
That whenever Bob Thought I WAS Ready,
That He (Duke) Would have me A Chanupa
Made — A Chanupa IS A Ceremonial
Pipe, Remember, We Showed you Bob's!
That really Surprised me, Because
I HAve never met DUKE. Duke is the
(SHAMAN?) Head MAN (Chief?). Evidently Bob
and Pepe have been TAlking to Him,
About Me. Bob Said, That Duke mAy
EVEN Try to come See me HERE!
About the Time We were TALKing about
This, I looked Across The Room, And
There WAS The Chaplain, HE GAUE
Bob A CARD, And SAiD HE could Do
It on a Spiritual ADUiSor BASiS!
Write Me & TEll me When you will Be
BACK AT Georgia's. I will CAll you There!
I Hope The Best for All of you!

I LOUE you All UERy Much!

Wade
H

64

3-12-03

HAPPY
BIRTH-
-DAY
RED

I LOVE YOU SIS
WADE

1-19-03

Hello JAKE

How is my Little buddy doing?
I hope you are doing great! I hope
you weren't to disAppointed (upset)
that it was too cold to go fishing. I WAS
really looking forwARD to TAking you and
TAylor fishing. Now, we already have
The fishing Poles at Georgia's, and
It will be WARM enough to go Next time!
I hope you geT to come BAck, AT least
once, in the next year. I should be out
for good then. Think Positive, keep a
STrong HeArT, and be the wonderful young
Man, ThaT I know you ARE!
If you ever WANT to TAlk, Just write me
a letter - I promise I'll Answer you
very FAST.   I love you very much JAKE

you will AlwAys be my Little Buddy 666

Love
uncle Wade

① 2-3-03

HAPPY 61ST
BIRTHDAY
MOM !!!
I LOVE
YOU
VERY MUCH

Wade

Nov. 24, 2002

Hello Hayley

How is School? I know you are doing better,
In school. You told me you would study more,
and I have no reason, not to Believe you.
I hope you are helping your Mom out, Since
your Grand Mother came back to ARKANSAS.
It WAS Great to See you, You are glowing
into a young lady. I hope when you grow up,
that you don't lose that sweet Peisonality, That I love
So much. I will love you Any way, but It would
be a Shame. Any one can be a hateful,
or disrespectful Grouch, It takes a little more effort
to be a Sweet heart! STudy Haid, and
Help your Mom, when you can. I love you
and miss you very much, Sweetheart!
I would like for you to White me a letter, and
let Me KNow what is going on, In your life!

                              I Love you
                              uncle WADE

P.S.
HAVE A HAPPY
ThanksGiving!

68

Nov. 24, 2002

Hello Jake

How is my Little Buddy? I hope you
are doing well. I hope you are still doing
Well In School. It is not Always easy to Study,
When you would rather be outside. Keep
doing good. Because It will pay off,
When you get older. ARE you and Your
DAd getting to Go DEER Hunting?
I hope So. Next January - (13 months)
I will be getting ready to come home. I Won't
Be long. I will be home for good, Before
you get out for Summer VACAtion Next year!
I promise you, We will have Some Great
Adventures. Hang in there, and keep a
strong Heart. You are a Wonderful young
Man, and I love you Very Much!!!

I love you

uncle Wade

P.S.
let me know what
is going on In your
life. HAVe a Great
Holiday!

①   Nov. 24, 02

What's up Red?

I was glad to get your E-Mail. I appreciate
you including Kim's E-mail, also. How is
the new Plan holding up? Is Robbie
working 6 days a week? I called Paul,
a few days ago, and he told me Robbie
didn't show, at Deer Camp. The Deer
weren't moving, because it was too warm!
Have you been keeping up, with the Hogs?
This year, Whoever wins the Boot Trophy,
will also win the West Championship.
Unless the Razorbacks self destruct (like vs Kentucky)
They should be playing Georgia, in Atlanta.
They play LSU, Friday at 1:30, in Little Rock.
- We are lucky it isn in Little Rock!!! Playing
There always Gives us an extra Edge!
I have to work Friday. We may get off
Early, but I don't know for sure. That will
be o.k., As long As we Win! I can always
watch the News, and the Houston Nutt show!
Mom Told me what happened with my Books.
It will be ok, Just Send them back to the Company.
They won't let me have them, If they come from
you. I looks like It will be some time
In January, Before I get a furlough.

70

They send Notices out to: ① The County
Sheriff ② The Chief of Police in that City
③ The Prosecutor who sent me to Prison.
This will TAKE About 10 DAys. Then
The Board has to meet, and Vote on ~~the~~
Letting me go. If they vote yes, they will set
me a Date. It will be a miracle, If all this
gets Accomplished, by the week end of the 21.st
They don't Allow furloughs, on ~~Holidays~~.
After the Initial furlough, It will go like
clock work - Every 30 dAys. I will be furloughing
to Georgia's. According to the ADC, thAt is
Mom's Address Also! Once I stArt getting
my furlough$, the time will go by, FAster.
Did you send in you and Robbie's Visitation
Forms? If you come to ArkAnSAs, for the
Holidays, you cAn get a speciAl visit. You cAn
get one on the wAy Here — And another
on the wAy BAck. I don't know If you
Realize how greAt It wAs to get to see the
BAbies! Even if I wAs disappointed that you
didn't get IN. I miss All of you very Much!!!

I love yAll with All My Heart & Soul.

WAD3

P.S. Please keep sending Me the B. MAYS!!

(1)

Hello Everyone

I had a good week Last week,
I hope you did Also. YOu know the
cold weather doesnt Bother me much.
The Cold Weather Makes me miss
A Good Warm Fire. I got down
Into The Teens and was even as low as
7 degrees in Little Rock — (9 degrees here)
on Friday Morning. I Was in it for about
a hour — yes It WAS cold!
I know I should have written this
Weekend — It is Partly Brad's Fault —
I read some of the Books he Sent
Me. AS FAR AS I know, My next
Furlough, will be on the Weekend, of
the 28th of February! I will Let you
know For Sure in Plenty of time!
Mom, I Think it is doing you good, to
be there. Enjoy the BAll Games, and
Just being close to the Kids! It Sounds
Like Hayley needs to start herself a
Daily Planner/organizer — So she can keep
her Activities straight, and Remember
Important Things!

Robbie, It probably wouldn't hurt to check out the finance job. Talk to Joe about it — He more than likely will hire you back, If It doesn't work out. Hopefully, I will be very close, If not already out, for Carson's Next Birthday. Jake, Even If you can't come in February, Me & you & Bob will go fishing soon d — I Promise — Maybe your Dad can come with us! Hayley, Hang In There, Adolescence only lasts a short while. It is easier, If you don't try to grow up too Fast b Keep It Together Red, Write me when you get a chance. I hope our Heavenly Father will watch over you all & keep you safe b

I Love you all very much bbb

page 1

Hello Sweetheart
— I hope you are doing fine. I'm O.K., I made
it through another week-end. There are only a couple
people left that came in with me. I should be on
the bus in the morning, headed for Pine Bluff.
If for some odd reason I don't make it in the
morning, I should definitely be on the Bus Friday
Morning. I will call Georgia at the Store as soon
as I get there, and get a chance to use the phone.
I will give her the address, so you can send me
a $20 dollar Money order. I will need shower shoes, a
bowl, Cup, and plastic forks & Spoons. I will also
get me some copies on my first Commissary order.
If they will let me, I am going to send my clothes &
tennis shoes to Georgia's Store C.O.D. I only have
an $11.00 check from Pulaski Co., I don't think that
will mail my clothes & Buy Shower Shoes.
I asked Debbie if you had brought any Dog food
by, she said No. I told her you probably
didn't go to Little Rock, last week-end. I
hope you didn't go up there, and forget
Bear's food. I got a letter from McKenna a few
minutes ago, No letter from Brad or Binky,
just some pictures that McKenna drew.
Kinda strange, but Sweet. I hope you had a
good week, without very much stress. Tell
Connie I said Hi — I will be so glad when
I get to talk to you, I love you & miss you
            very much WADE ———

Page 8.

Hello George —
How are ya — fine I hope!
Did you and Amy have lotsa fun?
Are you and Mom still walking? I forgot
to ask mom, in her part, if she remembered to
call uncle Butch. I hope someone did. If
not, call and tell him, that he is in my
prayers. I guess uncle Benny dropped
you off at Amy's on the way to Rodney's.
I hope they remember to take me a picture,
when they get done! I hope I will get
to talk to you tomorrow. I don't want to wait
here till Friday, but I might! Once I get
there (to prison) I will get visits the 1 + 3
Saturday of the month, I last for 4 hours. I
am only allowed 3 people at a time — you,
Mom, and Debbie first. You will have to
be there early — I think it is From 11:00 am til
3:00 pm — We get to go & sit in a Big room
with Food — so tell Mom to bring some
cash! oa I am going to go Now — I'll
talk to you soon — I Love you

WADE

Hello George,

I made it o.k. yesterday. I'm sorry I missed you, when I called. I called Mom last night, and she told me you sent me more money. She will give it back to you when she gets home, this weekend. I bet you will be glad when she gets back. I found out that only my immediate family can visit me, for the first 30 days. If you get this form back to them, and get approved before the 30 days are up, you can visit. I sent 1 form for you, & one for Mom. They need to be filled out and sent back to: Mrs. Tate c/o Visitation office, Cummins unit, P.O. Box 500, Grady, AR 71644-0500 The 0500 after the zip code will get the mail here faster. 4 people can visit at a time. My visitation for the 1st 60 days, is every other Saturday from 11:30 AM till 3:45 pm. I know this is a bad time of year for you, but maybe you can squeeze out 1 visit before Christmas. If not, we'll make up for it after Christmas — I hope you some idea how much your love and concern mean to me — I love you aunt Georgia —
Give uncle Benny a hug — I hope y'all have a nice Thanksgiving.

Love Wade

Sunday 18th

Hello George

I hope everything is well in your world.
This feels odd, writing with an ink pen. For 3½
months, I have had nothing to write with, but a
short pencil. Thank you very much, for sending
me that $50.00. I got it, that thursday, with your
1st letter. I got the 2nd letter, the next week. I really
appreciate you taking the time to think of me, and
write. I guess mom feels since she has
talked to me twice she doesn't need to write.
I'm just kidding, I know better. I didn't think
I would be here this long. I didn't even give her
the address — Don't you feel special?
I will have been here 2 weeks Monday.
Even though there is nothing to do, except Read & Eat,
these 2 weeks have went by fast. It is all downhill
from here. I will probably leave tomorrow (Mon)
I have delayed writing you, thinking I was leaving
that was silly, I could have just written another one.
I hope you can read this — I'm writing, sitting on
the side of my bunk — The Tables are always full of
people playing dominoes — (made out of Cardboard cracker Boxes)
I'm so close to getting to go outside & work, Watch TV, and
have 4 hour visits twice a month (for 1st two months) I can
deal with sitting here being bored! I'll call you
when I get to my unit! Give uncle Benny a Hug!
I Love y you!!!
WADE

P.S. Mom said she would give you the
$50.00 Back — I love you —

(2)

If I did have a letter, It was
probably the one you wrote of in the
letter, that you mailed 1/2 of to Mark —
The Money order was probably in it
also — I haven't gotten My 2 books from
Red yet, I will call her tonight to have
her check on them and wish them a
Happy New Year. I am going to call
Georgia, Also — I hope you are helping her
with the Phone Bill — It cost's her 40-50
dollars a month for me to call — I want
her to know, I will Be eligible for another
Visit, SATurday — Jan. 5. , In Amy's
letter to me, she volunteered to drive you,
if Georgia could not get away. She needs
to call and see if she has been approved
to Visit (Cummins unit Visitation office) You need
to get your act together, and come see me, I
don't care if you have to take A Bus + a cab
I haven't seen you in 4 months —
I hope you + Georgia were able to talk to
Jordon at least, if not see him —
Please Be careful and have a SAFE + HAPPY
New Year. I love you Mom —
WADE

6-12-03

Happy 37<u>th</u>
Birthday
Baby Brother!

You probably won't get this, until Monday. I'm sorry I didn't get your Birthday wishes to you on Time. Even Though It is a couple days late, I hope you realize how much you and your Family mean to me. I Love you all very much bbb I hope to be able to find some land, close enough to you and your Family, where we can develop a very close relationship. I would like to be close enough, to work with Taylor on his Baseball. I don't Think I would have any Trouble getting him to go fishing either. The only Problem, is That I don't like Janaya & her Family Being so FAR AWAY.

Mom Told me, That you said I could Parole out to you. That would be Great. While Living with you, I could easily Look at Alot of Land in The AREA. I could Also geT A Job easily & I am Thinking About Paroking (sp?) to Georgia. I can Transfer my Parole After 6 months. During That 6 months, I want to spend alot of Time with uncle Butch Honey! He told me, he would Teach me all He could, About Training Horses. Would It Be O.K. With you, If I were To move up There with you, After I have acquired some "Horse Sense." It Would only be for a Few MonthS. I need to figure a definite Plan out. I would be out in as Little as 4-5 months - all The way up to my I.E. DATE - April 21, 2004 - (only 10 months) My next Furlough is on The 27th, If you will write me a letter, telling me your BelT Size, I'll Bring your Birthday Present Home with me. I need to Know The Length to the center Hole, what you want on the BACK, and what color. Example mine is Brown w/ Gold Letters

HAPPY Birthday - I Love you All

WADE Very Much

General Commissary Order Form   Pulaski County Detention Facility

Name:_______________________   Trust Balance $___________

Book-In #___________ Unit___   Order Amount $___________

Food/Snacks/Candy/Mints

1001 Instant Lunch -Chicken	$0.91
1002 Instant Lunch -Shrimp	$0.91
1003 Instant Lunch -Beef	$0.91
1004 Instant Lunch -Picante	$0.91
1005 Andy Capp Salsa Fries	$0.49
1006 Andy Capp Hot Fries	$0.49
1007 Potato Chips	$0.49
1008 BBQ Potato Chips	$0.49
1009 Cajun Chips	$0.49
1010 Dill Chips	$0.49
1011 Corn Chips	$0.49
1012 BBQ Corn Chips	$0.49
1013 Chili Cheese Corn Chips	$0.49
1014 Nacho Tortilla Chips	$0.49
1015 Cheese Curls	$0.49
1016 Beef Sticks	$0.65
1017 Beef & Cheese Sticks	$0.65
1018 Hot & Spicy Sausage	$0.65
1019 Peanut Bar	$0.65
2020 M&M -Plain	$0.65
2021 M&M -Peanut	$0.65
2022 Butterfinger Bar	$0.65
2023 Snickers Bar	$0.65
2024 Nestles Crunch Bar	$0.65
2025 Payday Bar	$0.65
2027 Zero Bar	$0.65
2028 3 Musketeers Bar	$0.65
2029 Reese's Peanut Butter Cups	$0.65
2030 Hershey Bar with Almonds	$0.65
2031 Hershey Chocolate Bar	$0.65
2032 Nutrageous Bar	$0.65
2033 Kit Kat Bar	$0.65
2034 Skittles	$0.65
2035 Jolly Ranchers	$0.87
2036 Five Flavor Mints	$0.49
2037 Wintergreen Mints	$0.49
2038 Peppermint Mints	$0.49
2039 Spearmint Mints	$0.49

Cookies/Crackers/Pastry

3040 Chocolate Chip Cookie	$0.59
3043 Cheese/Peanut Butter Crackers	$0.54
3044 Banana Moon Pie	$0.70
3045 Chocolate Moon Pie	$0.70
3046 Honey Bun	$0.65
3047 Oatmeal Cake -Individual	$0.65
3048 Dunking Stix -Individual	$0.38
3049 Peanut Butter Bar -2 pk.	$0.49

Coffee/Beverages

4050 SS Tasters Choice -Decaf	$0.22
4051 SS Hills Bros. Coffee	$0.22
4052 Freeze Dried Columbian Coffee	$3.85
4053 Maxwell House Coffee	$3.85
4054 Instant Coffee -Decaf	$3.85
4055 SS Hot Cocoa	$0.28
4056 SS Orange Breakfast Drink	$0.28
4057 SS Tea with Lemon Drink	$0.28
4058 SS Fruit Drink	$0.28
4059 SS Cherry Drink	$0.28
4060 SS Lemonade Drink	$0.28
4061 Orange Drink	$1.25
4062 Lemonade Drink	$1.25
4063 Grape Drink	$1.25
4064 Tropical Punch Drink	$1.25

Tobacco Limit 10 Packs
Not Available for Units S/U

5065 Marlboro Red	$4.75
5066 Marlboro Light 100's	$4.75
5067 Winston 100's	$4.75
5068 Newport	$4.75
5069 Kool	$4.75
5070 USA Gold Regular	$3.70
5071 USA Gold Menthol	$3.70
5072 Top's Regular Rolling Tobacco	$2.00
5073 Top's Menthol Rolling Tobacco	$2.00
5074 Top's Rolling Paper	$1.07

Mail/Writing Materials

7164 Stamp	$0.34
6075 Large Stamped Envelope	$0.40
6076 White Envelope #10	$0.05
7165 Manila Envelope	$0.23
6077 Writing Pad -5x8	$1.02
6078 Legal Writing Pad -8 1/2x11	$1.28
6079 Pencil 4"	$0.08
6080 Eraser	$0.38

Miscellaneous

6081 Playing Cards	$2.00
6082 T-Shirt - Small	$3.36
6083 T-Shirt - Medium	$3.36
6084 T-Shirt - Large	$3.36
6085 T-Shirt - X-Large	$3.36
6086 T-Shirt - XX-Large	$4.43
6087 Underwear Briefs - 32	$2.79
6088 Underwear Briefs - 34	$2.79
6089 Underwear Briefs - 36	$2.79
6090 Underwear Briefs - 38	$2.79
6091 Underwear Briefs - 40	$2.79
6092 Underwear Briefs - 42	$2.79
6093 Boxer Shorts - Small	$3.75
6094 Boxer Shorts - Medium	$3.75
6095 Boxer Shorts - Large	$3.75
6096 Boxer Shorts - X-Large	$3.75
6097 Tube Socks - One Size Fits All	$1.56
6098 Thermal Top - Medium	$6.81
6099 Thermal Top - Large	$6.81
6100 Thermal Top - X-Large	$6.81
6101 Thermal Top - XX-Large	$8.41
6102 Thermal Bottom - Medium	$6.81
6103 Thermal Bottom - Large	$6.81
6104 Thermal Bottom - X-Large	$6.81
6105 Thermal Bottom - XX-Large	$8.41
6106 Bra - 34B	$4.80
6107 Bra - 36B	$4.80
6108 Bra - 38B	$4.80
6109 Bra - 40C	$4.80
6110 Bra - 42C	$4.80
6111 Bra - 44D	$4.80
6112 Bra - 36C	$4.80
6113 Women's Underwear - 5	$2.95
6114 Women's Underwear - 6	$2.95
6115 Women's Underwear - 7	$2.95
6116 Women's Underwear - 8	$2.95
6117 Women's Underwear - XL	$2.95
7168 Men's Canvas Shoes (sz. 8-14)	$8.55
7169 Women's Canvas Shoes (sz. 6-10)	$8.55

Personal Care

7118 Balsam Shampoo - Small	$1.02
7119 Balsam Conditioner - Small	$1.02
7122 Balsam Shampoo - Large	$2.41
7123 Balsam Conditioner - Large	$2.41
7124 Dandruff Shampoo	$1.23
7125 Sulfur 8 Shampoo	$3.53
7126 Normal Styling Gel	$2.46
7127 Black Orchid Hair Food	$2.46
7128 Black Orchid Pomade	$2.14
7129 Black Orchid Curl Activator	$2.46
7130 Coco Butter Cream	$1.02
7131 Men's Stick Deodorant	$2.56
7132 Women's Stick Deodorant	$2.56
7133 Baby Powder	$1.02
7135 Baby Oil	$1.02
7136 Baby Lotion	$1.02
7137 Skin Care Lotion	$2.14
7141 Petroleum Jelly	$2.46
7142 Original Skin Cream	$2.14
7144 Alcohol Free Mouthwash	$1.82
7145 Irish Spring Soap	$1.46
7147 Dial Soap	$1.46
7148 Tone Coca Butter Soap	$2.14
7149 Close-Up Toothpaste	$1.93
7150 Colgate Toothpaste	$2.02
7151 Toothbrush	$0.26
7152 Toothbrush Holder	$0.90
7153 Effergrip	$4.05
7154 Disposable Razor	$0.38
7155 Douche - Twin Pack	$1.93
7156 Tylenol Extra Str. - 2 pk	$0.70
7158 Advil - 2 pk	$0.70
7160 Halls	$0.91
7161 Comb - 5"	$0.28
7162 Comb - 7"	$0.59
7163 Shower Cap	$0.33
7166 Contact Lens Cleaner	$5.80
7167 Contact Lens Case	$1.26
7170 Wave Cap	$2.52
7171 Anti-Perspirant Deodorant	$2.56
7172 Magic Shave Cream	$3.78
7173 Denture Cleanser - Tablets	$6.52
7174 Vitamins - 100 Per Bottle	$3.95

Damages or shortages must be identified upon delivery to you. If you are released or transferred prior to receiving your order, the price of the commissary you requested will be credited to your account and a check will be issued and mailed to the address listed on your book-in sheet. By signing below, I acknowledge and understand the terms of commissary orders and authorize funds to be deducted from my trust account to pay for this order. All sales are final.

Signature

____

Date

____

Prices effective 07/23/01

2-10-04

Hello Aunt Georgia

I hope you are doing well Today.
I Know It will mean, you will be Tired again,
but I hope you all are still Busy.
I am sending you my W-2 Forms, do
whatever you Think Dest — Either
try to do my Taxes on Line, or Wait
Until I get out. Mom Said, that If
I don't have to pay anything, I
wouldn't have to pay a Penalty.
Please check into That — I would hate
to have to pay a penalty, when a Phone
call, or letter, could get me an extension!
Uncle Benny, Thanks, — I Know That
Aunt Georgia will probably get your assistance.
Thanks for Everything That Both of you
Do, I Love you Both Very Much!

HAPPY VALENTINES

DAY, Georgia

I Love you
WADE

82

5-8-03

HAPPY MOTHER'S DAY !!!

MOM & GEORGIA

To Both of you Wonderful Womens
By the time you get This, I will
have already called. We got our
furlough's BACK. Mine is scheduled
for May the 16th. I cAlled Janaga
last night. What are you doing about
Carson? I probably will be Changing
Jobs at work, I bid on an opening
in the Warehouse. I have been
Working from 6:00 Am to 3:30 Pm All
week. I will call Tomorrow —

I love you Both Very Much!

P.S. I LOVE you   WadE
Too, UNCle Benny — But This
   IS A MoThers DAy Letterd

83

12/31/01

Hello Mom,

I hope you have had a Happy Holiday Season, considering the Damper I have put on it. Next christmas I will be there, either from a 48 hr furlough (work-release), on a 5 day furlough ("309"). I got very tickled at you, when I was reading your last letter, I got one page of Mark's letter, he must have got the second page of mine. I got good cards & letters from all the Whiteheads, even Randy. Bobby & Leucienia both apologized for not having written more often. They shouldn't feel that way, just because that damn place I was in wouldn't let me mail but 2 letters a week, one went to you & georgia + the other went to Debbie & Landon - I had to Neglect the others, It wasn't their fault. I still haven't found out, if my "309" slot at Dumas is 100% Guaranteed - I will find out this week, though. Have you talked to Sheriff Bishop to See if he might want me there? If he is interested, I would like to know what living conditions his "309"s Get - I went out to Yard Call Friday Afternoon, I was told my name was Called, during mail Call, But they didn't leave a letter -

1-19-03

Hello Hayley

I'm glad you made It home Safely.
Did you Enjoy your Trip? I hope so!
It WAS gleat to see you, for a whole
weekend. I hope I get to see
you and your fAmily, on at least
one more of my weekends, Before
I get out for good. I don't WANT a
whole year to go By, without seeing
you again. Please be the sweet
young lady, that I know you are.
Keep Tlying hard in school, and help
your Mom, as much as you CAN.
I love you very much HAyley.

Love & Kisses
uncle WADE

P.S. I would like
To Hear from
you, every Now
and then.

85

Hello George

Didn't want to pass up a chance
to say Thank you. I appreciate
everything you do, probably more than
you understand. I'll see you and
Uncle Benny soon —

Have a Good Day

I love you

Wade

Good Morning Mom

It's Friday morning, and since my
Boss didn't come get me for work, I
thought It would be a good time to
write some letters. My Boss told me
Wednesday, that he put me up for a
job change. After learning that, and
talking to Georgia, I put in a request, to
talk with Mis Woods. Mis. Woods is the
Classification Lady. I should go up in front
of the classification Board Tuesday, the 9th.
Hopefully, after talking to the Child Support
Investigator, Mis Woods will let me have
my 1-B Trusty, Even if they don't get Verification,
By Tuesday. Then I can put in my Application
for work-Release & "309", and ride Cowboy
on the Beef-Herd until Work-Release comes
to get me. I talked to my friend yesterday
Afternoon, And he told me the only person,
they were putting A hold on, in the Beef-
Herd, was the person who shoed the Horses.
I probably won't get to talk to her Monday,
But I will learn something on Tuesday,
either way. Thank you for the money,
I haven't gotten it yet, but it will get here
Before I run out.

I'm glad you are going to take
care of Bear's Heart Worm Medicine.
It would devastate me, if Something
happened to him, while I am locked up.
I have been the only constant in his life,
Now he doesn't know what happened to me,
or where I have gone. Debbie Said
that he still searches for me, every time
Some one pulls up, at the house. It
took her forever to get him to eat
Properly. It is comforting that he has
accepted her So well.
I am thankful, that you have a job,
that pays you so well, It is even better,
that you don't have to drive. I believe,
It will work out, that I will be in a work-
release, about the time your Job runs out.
That way you can go spend Some time,
with Red, without worrying So much, about
Money. I missed being with you this
past week-end, but hopefully, I'll get to see you
Soon. I love you very much —

WADE

Good Morning George

Just when I think I will never be
able to show you how much I Appreciate
everything you have done, you do Something
else, that never fails, to make me feel
like the luckiest person on Earth!
Some people don't even get the Wonderful
feeling of I mother's unconditional love,
And God has blessed me with three —
even though he has taken one from me,
I am still one of the richest and most Blessed
people ever! I don't mean to sound,
like I am not AWARE of, and appreciate,
how much my mother loves me —
But She IS my Mother, When I think
of the pain, and stress that I have brought
upon both of you, It makes me cry!
I hope to see you Soon. I love
very Much —

WADE

3-29-02

Hello George

HAPPy EASTeF

I hope you aren't wearing yourself
down, working too Hard on these taxes!
How is your new Truck working out?
I hope you like it. Tell Rodney not
To worry About Me, that much. If he
CAme to Visit, Before he WAS finished,
his Body would be here, but Not his heart + mind.
Do you think we might could get him to
give you a SATurdAy Morning off —
After he is through with his Truck, of Course
I'm going to Cut this short so I can
get it in the mail, on the WAy to Chow.
It's Almost 10:00 AM — They ARe LiAble
to CAll Chow Any minute — Give uncla
Beany A hug —
    I Love You   —

                    W.A.B.

90

3-29-02

Hello Mom
        HAPPY EASTER
I Hope you have been doing fine this week!
I know you aren't used to working a full
week yet, I don't know if I will be
seeing you Tomorrow, or not. I haven't called
Georgia yet. I'll call her this Afternoon.
I was so sore yesterday, that I didn't want
to get out of Bed. I went out on the yard
Wednesday Afternoon, I walked 4 miles,
As fast As I could walk, thats pretty fast.
I also did some Push-ups. I enjoyed it
Very much. It was a Beautiful Afternoon,
and I put my head phones on, and took off
walking. I had to work Thursday, so
I had to Tough it out & set up. I was glad
to get off early - (about 11:00 pm). I went
to Bed to Read - and ended up sleeping until
6:00 pm. I got my Books from Janasa
and Brad on the same day - Wednesday.
Janasa sent me 2 more - But Brad surprised
me, with the whole "AREA 51" series - He
had Already sent me one of them, & He
sent me the other 5. Yes I called & Thanked
Him
         I LOVE YOU &
            WADE

3-18-02

Hello Mom:

I hope you ARE well. I am doing
fine. At this moment I am sitting
at the table, writing this letter, and
listening to my new Sony WALKMAN.
I bet I have a wide grin on my
face. Thank YOU for sending the extra
money. You can think of this AS my
Birthday present, I didn't realize
How much I had missed my music.
This was the best $22.00 you have
spent in a while. I had a wonderful
visit SATurday. It was so good to
see Paul & Marlon. Bob & Shelley
CAME Also. I don't know what Bob
did to get Shelley to come — She is
Always tired — working All week &
taking care of Her flower Garden!
I sure miss you a lot Georgia — I hope
you CAN come this SATurday!
I still have $50.00 left, that should
last me 2 weeks. Paul told me about
some kind of lost ($200.00) Associated with
my child support case. It must be
court cost. Don't work to HARD!
I miss you & love you VERy Much

WADE

I love you — wade

3-18-02

Hello George — Give Benny a Aug

I Hope you and uncle Benny are
Doing Good, I think I made a wise
choice on my Radio — not only was it
$2.50 cheaper, but it uses only 1 AA
Battery Instead of 2 AAA, like the
AIWA. A Few Guys have told me that the
Sony will pick up more stations Also

   I don't Know Any thing about the Inline
6 cylinder motor. As A Rule, 6 Cylinders
last a long Time — They don't develop RPM's AS FAST
They Also deliver a lot of Torque — for Towing.
Plus 275 HP is more than my '97
350 Put out — That Should Be a good
Combination. The main Thing Is the
fact that I Know How many Safety
features they have — Remember how hard
I hit that Tree in my '97 — Without my
Seat Belt! You made a very wise choice.
I Am mailing you a visitation form + Landon
one Also, I Know It won't Be in time
for Him to come this Saturday, But If
He Hurries + Gets It Sent Back — He Can
Come Next Time! I'll Call you Friday
Thanks for Everything — I Hope to see you
Saturday — I miss you + mom

   I love you — Wade

Front
My Truck

93

MAY 1, 2002

Good Morning George

I hope your back is Better. Maybe
that new medicine will work well, for you!
The main thing you have to do is realize,
that, for a month or 2, at least, you will
have to be especially careful. Don't
overdo it, don't lift anything, that you
don't absolutely have to, and don't stay in
uncomfortable positions, for very long at
one time.
I hope Rodney & Uncle Benny got all
the bugs worked out of the truck, in time,
for Rodney to leave today.
I will be forever grateful to you, for everything,
you have done to help me, while I have been
incarcerated. You have helped me in so many
ways. Thank you for calling Bob, and
for thinking of Debbie & Bear. He
will get Bear's medicine as soon as he
feels better. Hopefully, they won't hold
me back, from going to work release, very
long. I am the only Electrician they
have, in outside Maintenance, right now.
Please take Extra care with your back!
I'll call you today!

I Love You WADE!

Happy Pre-Mother's Day

94

May 1, 2002

Good Morning Mom

Well, I don't feel 40 YEARS old! I Guess
It is better, than feeling older, than my years!
You know how I always Say, The lord works
in mysterious ways. Here is one more
example. You are aware, of how I used to
refuse, to work on my birthday. I put in my
Sick-call request, to go to the Nurse, and get
my weekly Sinus Medicine, It can take, from
2 - 7 days, to get put on Sick-call, from
the time you put in a request. I put my
request in Sunday, I am laid in all day,
for Sick-call. That means I don't have to
go to work. I told you, that I don't buy
Ice cream on the Store, during the week.
I save that for a treat, during visitation. I am
going to splurge today - since Monday &
Wednesday are store days out here.
I can't have a birthday cake & Ice cream,
but I can have a pint of Ice cream &
an apple or cherry pie (Individual Pastry).
It could be alot worse, Plus I will
get to talk to Georgin this Afternoon -
Thank you for the $100.00 - I was down to
$1.35. I know you are going to be
finished, with your Job, on May 10th.

I don't remember, if you are coming
to visit, this weekend, or the next.
Bob & Shelley came to visit me Saturday.
It was a nice surprise to see Shelly. Bob
did not look well. They are not supposed to
come visit this week-end, but you can't ever
tell about Bob! I talked to Tanya a
few days ago, but I have been unable
to catch Brad & Family, at home. I also
tried to call Paul a couple times. I will
try to get ahold of Brad, later today.
It has been 2 weeks (almost), since I put
in my Application for Work-Release. I have
been told that it can take, up to a month,
to get confirmation, of Approval, back.
Didn't you tell me, that your current Boss,
is 2nd in charge of Work-Release. If so,
He might be willing, to help me obtain a good
Job, at a good location! I guess I am not
getting too old — I still heal quickly. I
was only laid-up for 1 day, after I sprained
my shoulder, it's still sore, but not so bad,
that it has kept me from working. I didn't want
to, but I kept myself out of the Softball game
on Sunday. I didn't need to make it worse!
TAKE CARE of Yourself — I Love You!

WADE

4-10-02

To: My Two Precious Ladies!

I Love & Miss you Both Very
Much! I hope that both of you
realize, that these CARDS dont even begin
to Express, how much I Love & Appreciate
The Both of you! George I wish the
~~Butterflies~~ Butterflies were bigger.
I had planned for them to be drawn
instead of flowers — oh well. —
I hope you are Both very pleased,
With your CARDS.
   Mom told me in her letter, that you
were down In your back, Please
Take Good CARE of Yourself! I Tried
to CALL Tuesday — between 5:00 & 5:30ᵗ
you must have been gone to eat. I Tried
to CALL today, and none of my Phone
numbers worked. I found out later
that the Phone system is on the
Blink — let's hope they fix it quickly!
I Am still on inside Maintenance — I went Before
the CLASSIFICATION board Tuesday.
The ASSISSTAnt Worden wen'T let me outside
the fence, until Cummins gets the
Paperwork, to pull the detainer, from
Independance Co sheriffs Dept.
    I Love you Both Very Much
            WADE

P.S. I'll write again this week-end
It wouldn't hurt to call the Independance Co- Sheriffs Dept.

2-17-02

Hello Mom, Hello George

I hope you are Both doing well,
I Also hope you haven't been worried,
since I haven't called this week. Monday
Is a Holiday, the mail won't run until
Tuesday, Maybe I need to stop calling
so much, how much IS it costing you
a month - $40 -50. Thank you very much
for my letter, and my money-order; yes you
can send a money order for any Amount you
want. I am sure both of you are aware,
of how much I enjoyed your visit.
I am going to try every thing I can to get
my visitation Day switched to Sunday!
I feel Bad enough for all the Pain I
have caused, with adding more stress
over financial sacrifices. I still can't Believe
uncle Benny Agreed to close the store.
I'll write you ladies another letter this
week - Yes I'll call Also -
I hope you have luck with Krissy - Soon

P.S
I Am tempted to
Buy A Radio - But,
I. Better wait until
I get A little more
Ahead. Thanks
for everything

I love you Both very Much

Tuesday 12/11/01

Hello Mom,
   I have been putting off writing my
letters, because my light bulb blew
out Sunday night. It is After 3:00pm
Tuesday, and I still don't have a light Bulb.
I had an all day lay-in from work, because of
being on Sick-Call - Things move so slow
around here, I have been waiting to see
the doctor, since the 1st day I got here,
November the 19th. I have seen the Nurse
1 time during each week, except the 1st - Thanksgiving,
They Just give me some Ibuprofen, and Chlor-Trimeton
and tell me to keep watching the LAY-In list.
I can't get my prescription for Naprosyn, until I
see the doctor.
   The rules here State, that if the temperature is
42° F. or colder, the Hoe squads don't go outside
to work. I think their Thermometer is Broken.
They called us out to work yesterday morning
and this morning Also. I believe it was below
42°F both mornings. They must be trying to get
the rest of the vegetables and pecans in, before
the weather turns bad for good. I got a letter
from Bob yesterday, so I called him. I told him to
go ahead & sell the 80 Acres. He is trying to come
visit Saturday, Also, Remember to bring a few dollars
for cokes & snacks, & dinner during visitation. I
gotta go. It's getting dark - I love you.

Tuesday 12/11/01

Hello Mom,
I have been putting off writing my
letters, because my light bulb blew
out Sunday night. It is After 3:00pm
Tuesday, and I still dont have a light Bulb.
I had an all day lay-in from work, because of
being on Sick-Call - Things move so slow
around here, I have been waiting to see
the doctor, Since the 1st day I got here,
November the 19th. I have seen the Nurse
1 time during each week, except the 1st - Thanksgiving,
They Just give me some Ibuprofen, and Chlor-Trimeton
and tell me to keep watching the LAY-In list.
I cant get my prescription for Noprosyn, until I
see the doctor.
The rules here State, that if the temperature is
42°F. or colder, the Hoe Squads dont go outside
to work. I think their Thermometer is Broken,
They called us out to work yesterday morning
and this morning Also. I believe it was below
42°F both mornings. They must be trying to get
The rest of the vegetables and pecans in, before
the weather turns bad for good. I got a letter
from Bob yesterday, so I called him. I told him to
go ahead & Sell the 80 Acres. He is trying to come
Visit Saturday, Also, Remember to bring a few dollars
for cakes & Snacks, & dinner during Visitation. I
gotta go. It's getting dark - I love you.

Hello George

I hope you will read Mom's letter also, because it's getting dark. I'll have to be short & sweet, before the Sun goes down. I didn't call Rodney this week-end, figured I would let it get closer to Christmas. ~~That is~~ The last thing I want, is for him to feel uncomfortable, when he looks at his phone bill. This is the last week, of my 30 day waiting period. I wish you, or mom, would CALL the VISITATION office, and remind them. Next month I WANT my 2 regular VISITATIONS. I am going to get very upset if I CAN'T, because some Idiot hasn't done her, or HIS, Job. Debbie CALLed yesterday, the lady she talked to, told her she WAS busy, and didn't have time to check on iT — to CALL her back that B.S. will not WORK — I have decided I want to find some land between Heber & Batesville. I have also figured out your surprise, I know It's mean to make you wait 2 years — If you really want to know, I will probably break down —

I love you Georgia

WADE

P.S. Give uncle Benny a Hug & remind mom to bring a few dollars CASH for VISITATION.

She may want to bring a money order, too — It's up to her.

①   Sun 6-2-02

Hello Mom + Red ?

I am combining your Letters. I don't
want to ~~want to~~ write this Info Twice!
Thanks for your Letters & E-mails.
Red, I am glad that you Just forgot to order
those Books. I didn't want you to have
paid for them, and them be lost somewhere.
    I had 2 days off this week - Wednesday +
Saturday. I will get one day off Next week.
My work schedule, will work like that, until
I leave for Work-Release. I should get
Interviewed (They can't screened) during
the First part of this month. After I
have been screened, and approved, It
shouldn't Take A month After that. I
should be at a Work-Release center, by
no later than August. August 9th will
be A year & I figure the next year will
go by a lot faster. I will be working
At A real Job, Making Money, and getting
one week-end a month at home. My
Week-end in December may not be
around Christmas, but It will Be close
enough. I know I have a Cushy Job Now,
But I am still Impatient, to get to Work-
Release —

I had a very good visit Saturday. Debbie's mom, and a friend of hers, brought Debbie, and dropped her off. They went shopping in Pine Bluff, and Picked her up at 3:00 Pm. We had 3½ hours to visit. She is looking alot better. She has gained about 5 lbs. After My visit, I decided my shoulder was ready for a test Run. I started early, since the handball court was empty, and I could get in a little practice. My shoulder didn't bother me, near as much as my extra 25 lbs. I still did alright for a fat Boy, HAd that hasn't played since the early 80's. I won 1 and lost 3. Yes the last three were against good players. I got a very good sweaty work out — thats what I wanted. I think I will spend the money, for a pair of tennis shoes, when my next money gets here — Remember my Boots — thats what I played in. I phaN on Playing Again this Afternoon, to work out the stiffness! I figure I can get Back in fair shape, in the next 6-8 weeks! I want to be in better shape for work — Released, I love & miss you All very Much — ooo

Dad

Hello HAyley

Thank you for your Letter, and your pretty drawing. I glad you like your necklAce. The main thing is for you to Remember How much your uncle Wade Loves you! Your Mom SAid that you picked up the GAme, of Soft bAll, very Quickly. I knew you would. You Are a Spunky, enersetic young Lady. Your Mom said that your bAby brother wAs getting as FAt, As a PiG. That means he is good and healthy!

I hope you have a Wonderful Summer, and a SAfe one. I think I may get to See you Soon - Be a good Girl -

I MISS you and I Love you VERy much!!!

uncle WADE

①   Friday 6-14-02

Hello Mom. & Red

    Yes, you two ARE going to have to
share a letter. I don't want to write
all this down twice. I got Both letters,
The letter with the money order, I recieved
yesterday, Thank you. I thought that was
cute, that JAKE wanted to keep his letter private.
I hope the little pistol, didn't have any
trouble, reading my handwriting. Thank you
For the Computer Pictures. Boy, you
woren't Kidding, about CARSON being a
little butterbALL. When are y'all coming
to ARKANSAS? ARE JAKE and hAyley
coming to see me Also? What are you
going to do with CARSon while you
come Visit? What Do you cAll him,
CARSon or CARSon Wade? I got
the paper, telling me that handon is
Approved, to Visit. Before y'all come,
Please remember, to cAll the Visitation
office, and make sure you are on the list'd
He,(hAndon) and Geolgia, Rodney, might come
with them, ARe going to come Visit Soon. I
to Remember to tell GeoJgia, that he is Approved,
When I (All this Afternoon. I didn't get
to talk to her, last Friday, they were gone t
Indianapolis, Indiana,

105

⓪

Rodney had a CAR Show there.
He did good. He got another award.
I called him Monday night. I will try
and get ahold of Brad, this Afternoon.
I hope you remembered to call Him.
I still don't know which Work. Release,
I Will go to. I did find out, that Pine Bluff
doesn't come and screen Applicants in Person.
They Just come get you. I asked Brad
to check on the one 'in Springdale. He
Can call and find out all the Information.
It's small, but the Jobs are good, and so
is the Pay. The only Negative thing, Is,
that it is so far away, from every one else.
I Will just be glad, to be back making
money. I have from 18-21 months left,
If I can Save a minimum, of $500.⁰⁰ a month,
I should have between, $9,000.⁰⁰ + $11,000.⁰⁰.
I should be able to pay cash for a truck, and
have some Left over. Robbie said he could
help me find one. I should be Able to get
a used Mazda 4x4 for less than $10,000.
I Will need something, dependable, good on Gas,
and 4x4, I won't care what it Looks like,
or how fast it runs. I will need it to run alot
of miles, as cheap as possible. The 4x4 will
Be A must. I Miss You + Love You
Both Very Much. Dad

106

Sunday 9-22-02

Hello Sis

I don't know if Mom is still there,
if she is, she can read this also. I hope
I hope things have smoothed out, for you.
I think it was a wise decision for Robbie,
to go to finance school. I told him that a
long time ago. As a finance person, he
will make money, on the contracting of all the sales.
He will also be out of the politics of management.

I guess Mom has told you of my job, it was
tough. It was very hot and physically demanding. I
have lost between 5 & 10 pounds, but more importantly,
I have gotten alot of my stamina back. Wednesday
morning I had a very heated argument, with the
free-world black man, that I worked with. Tuesday
afternoon, my boss told me to come into work 2 hours
early (at 5:00 Am), I was to hang clean shirts on the
line. He tried to tell me to get to work on the
mats. I told him to leave me alone, he wasn't my
boss, and I knew, what I was supposed to do.
He got in my face, and I instantly reacted. He is
not in jail, so he has nothing to lose, except his job.
Very quickly, another inmate (black) talked him
down. As he left, he said he would get me.
At 7:00 Am, I went to the mat area to go to
work. He told me to leave, that he didn't
need me back there.

107

I told him he had no say so, in where
I worked. I realized real quick, that I
was about to lose control, And hit him.
I told him he was very lucky, that, I was
in JAil, and couldn't Afford to beat his
Ass. I turned around and walked off.
I went to the Bosses office. They Arrived about
7:15 Am. I told them what had happened, and
If they didn't handle the Situation, that I would.
I was not putting up with Someone threatening
me! The boss talked to both of us. Told us to
do our Job, and leave each other alone. To not
even speak to each other. The next dAy they
moved me to a Janitorial Job. The lord works in
Mysterious ways. He tested me, I passed, He
rewarded me. I like my new Job. I have
a lot of different responsibilities, and time goes
by very quickly. I do a lot of walking, but I
ordered me a pair of Doc Marten work boots.
They were 109.⁰⁰ minus a 10% discount. I wiy
have to leave them at work, in my locker. They
should be very comfortable. I make 7.00/HR,
and get any where from 40, to 55 hrs. My normal
HRS. are from 7:00 am to 3:30 am.

I had 2 visits Saturday. Bob
and Debbie came first, and Georgia and
Rodney came at 2:30 P.M. I really enjoyed
seeing Georgia, and Rodney. I tried to call,
but your phone doesn't cooperate anymore. I
can't talk to you, so please keep sending
me copies of your e-mails. Tell Hayley
and Jake how much I miss & love them.
If Mom is still there, she knows how much I
love her, just give her a kiss for me. Mom, Please
be extra careful, not to let the baby distract
you while you're driving. I can't have anything
happen to either one of you b well, I
am going to go take a shower, & shave, and
get ready for church. I love and miss
you all very much b&b Yes, Robbie, even
you - #8

Friday 6-14-02

<u>Hello JAKE!</u>

I hope you have been having
Fun playing basebALl. You sure
do look sharp in the pictures
you sent me. The pictures of you
playing baseball. I hope you
and your friends, have a good place
to play, close to your houses. Hopefully,
you will be coming to see me soon.
You can tell me all about it then.
Bob has left to go to the big
Indian Dance. It is called the
Sun Dance. It is a very Big thing.
It last about a week, It is a Dance
that praises God, and all he Gives us
through the Sun. Not everyone Dances.
The Dancers will Dance Night and Day,
for 4 days. The Dancers Don't
Eat or Drink for the whole 4 days.
Then Everyone Joins the Dancers in a feast.
Summer after Next, Maybe your Mom,
will let you go with me and Bob,
to a real Sundance, Ask your Mom,
She might find you a book on Native
American Dances. I hope to see you
Soon. I miss you & I Love You very much &
                    Uncle Warde

Sunday 6-2-02

Hello Jake

Thank you for your drawing. I hope you like your necklace. It is a real Indian Arrow head. The small ones, like that one were mostly used for ceremonies. They are called Bird Points, But real Arrow heads, for shooting Birds, were Blunt + rounded instead of sharp pointed,

Bird Point

— Regular Hunting Point

That way they would knock a Bird down, But were less likely to Be damaged, or lost in the Trunk of A Tree.

Your Mom told me you did real well in Baseball. I knew you would get over being hit in the nose, by that Ball — I hope you have a very fun summer. I may get to see ya'll soon — Be careful, and stay safe —

I Love you very much

Uncle Wads

Friday 6-14-02

Hello Hayley

How are you? I hope you are doing
as well, As you look in you pictures.
From those pictures you sent me, it looks
like you are rapidly becoming, a Beautiful
young Lady. If you are careful, not
to act without thinking, you'll be Surprised
how easy It will be, to keep from doing things,
you will be ashamed of later! Always
keep your head up, and be very proud of
who you are. You are very special, there
is not another person like you.
I am glad that you enjoyed Softball.
It is Always good to broaden your experiences
in life. That is the way you find out what
you like and what you don't b I hope
y'all are enjoying your Summer to the fullest.
I hope to get to See you Soon, and you
can tell Me all about it. Help your mom
and your Mimi - So you can all Have fun b
I miss you and Love you very much bbb

Uncle WADE

Thursday June 27, 2002

Hello JAKE

I Hope my Little Buddy is doing Well.
ARE you having a fun Summer? I'm
Sorry we didn't get to Visit, When you CAME
to Arkansas. I think they will have every
thing Straigtened out, by the time you Come
Back, I hope you have a SAFe 4th of July
Holiday. Be cAreful with those Fireworks!
   Bob got BACK from the Indian Sun
Dance, on Sunday. He was very tired.
Did you have your Mom find you Some
Information, on The Sun Dance? I am
almost ½ done being in Jail. I only
have to be awAy from ya'll, for one more Summer.
Be A Good Boy. I'll See you Soon.
   I Love you Very much bbb

                              Uncle Wade

5-20-02

Happy Birthday Jake

I hope you had A Great
Birthday. Mimi will Be Bringing
your present with her. I hope you
like it. I didn't Buy it, I found it, and
it is hand made afterward. I'm Sorry
we didn't get to talk long, because
you were in the bath tub. I will
be CAlling this week end, we can
talk some more then. I hope you
ARe having fun PlAying Baseball.
You will be out of school for
Summer VACAtion Soon, I hope you
have a fun Summer. We have this
Summer and one more, before we can
START Some Serious fishing. It will
Be over Before you know it, And I'll
Be Home — Be a Good Boy
This Summer — I miss youd

I Love you Very Much JAKE

uncle WADE

114

Hello Mom & Red

I am glad you had a SAFe trip to ARKANSAS. I wish things had worked out, where I could have seen you all. Before you come next time, call the visitation office. YOU could call and hurry them Now, so when you get to come, you will already Be cleared. When you call them, ask them about out-of-state visitation. I still havent recieved the letter with all the computer pictures. Did you put all the correct Information on there?

Everything is running smoothly here, I still havent heard anything from any of the work-Release people. Brad called the one In springsdale. After telling him, "SiR we usually dont have people calling us like this," the lady gave him the Information. They have the BesT paying Jobs, But only 42 Beds. There is a 60 or 90 day probation period, Before furloughs are started. It might Be Inconvenient to be WAy up there, But If they are 1st to offer, I'm gone & I Hope you have a SAFe 4th of July Holiday. I Still have between 50-60 dollars. Thats good for 1 week + shoes, or Two weeks — I miss you + love you very much too

Wade

Hello Hayley

Did you get to come to Arkansas? It is always fun to come, and visit People you have not seen, in a long time. Hopefully, I will get to see you this Summer. I hope you Enjoy, the Rest of your Summer. Be a good girl, and Do your part to help every thing run smoothly. Be careful, and stay safe over the Holiday (4th of July). I miss you, and I Love you very much Hayley б ₽ see you soon.

4-7-02

Hello Hayley

I hope everything is OK in your World, I know It gets Hectic this time of year. With school getting ready to end, and Sports starting up, I bet you are a very busy young Lady. Do you play Softball, or just Soccer. Dont Limit yourself, broaden your experiences. You will only be young once, So be the Smart young Lady I know you to be, and obtain the most out of It. As you get older, Your Life will get even more Interesting. Keeping a strong Sense of Respect ① for yourself ② for others — Will help you alot.

Be CAREFUL, and help your Mom WAtchout, for your Brothers. Babies CAN get into alot of mischief, And get hurt, because they dont know any better!

I Miss you & I Love you very Much ooo

Uncle WADE

4-10-02

To: My Two Precious Ladies!

I Love & Miss you Both Very
Much! I hope that both of you
Realize, that these CARDS dont even begin
to Express, how much I Love & Appreciate
The Both of you! George I wish the
~~~~~~ Butterflies were bigger.
I had planned for them to be drawn
instead of flowers — oh well —
I hope you are Both very pleased
with your CARDS,
Mom told me in her letter, that you
were down in your back. Please
Take good CARE of Yourself! I Tried
to CALL Tuesday — between 5:00 & 5:30ᵖ
you must have been gone to eat. I Tried
to CALL today, and none of my Phone
numbers worked. I found out later
that the Phone System is on the
Blink — let's Hope they fix it quickly!
I am still on 'inside Maintenence — I went Before
the CLASSIFICATion board Tuesday.
The Assisstant Worden won't let me outside
the fence, until Cummins gets the
Paperwork, to pull the detainer, from
Independence co sheriffs Dept.

S. I'll write again this week-end
I wouldn't want to coM the Independence Co- sheriff Dept.

118
~~~~~~

Tuesday 12/11/01

Hello ~~Dear~~ My Two precious ~~ladies~~
I have been putting off writing my
letters, because my light bulb blew
out Sunday night. It is After 3:00pm
Tuesday, and I still dont have a light Bulb.
I had an all day lay-in from work, because of
being on Sick-CAll - Things move So Slow
around ~~hell~~, I have been waiting to see
the doctor, Since the 1st day I got here,
November the 19th. I have Seen the Nurse
1 time during each week, except the 1st - Thanksgiving,
They Just give me Some Ibuprofen, and Chlor-Trimeton,
and tell me to keep wAtching the LAY-In list.
I can't get my prescription for Naprosyn, until I
See the doctor.
The rules here State, that if the temperature is
42° F. or colder, the Hoe squads dont go outside
to work. I think their Thermometer is Broken,
They called us out to work yesterday morning
and this morning Also. I believe it wAs below
42°F both mornings. They must be trying to get
The rest of the vegetables and pecans in, before
the weather turns bad for good. I got a letter
from Bob yesterday, so I called him. I told him to
go ahead & Sell the 80 Acres. He is trying to come
visit saturday, Also, Remember to bring a few dollars

I don't remember, If you are coming
to visit, this weekend, or the next.
Bob & Shelley came to visit me Saturday.
It was a nice surprise to see Shelly. Bob
did not look well. They are not supposed to
come visit this week-end, but you can't ever
tell about Bob! I talked to Javaga a
few days ago, but I have been unable
to catch Brad & Family, at home. I also
tried to call Paul a couple times. I will
try to get ahold of Brad, Later today.
It has been 2 weeks (Almost), since I put
in my Application for Work-Release. I have
been told that it can take, up to a month,
to get confirmation, of Approval, back.
Didn't you tell me, that your current Boss,
is 2nd in charge of work-Release. If so,
He might be willing, to help me obtain a good
job, at a good location! I guess I am not
getting too old - I still heal quickly. I
was only laid-up for 1 day, after I sprained
my shoulder, It Is still sore, but not so bad,
that it has kept me from working. I didn't want
to, but I kept myself out of the soft ball game
on Sunday. I didn't need to make it worse ♂
Take care of yourself — I Love You ♂

3-18-02

Hello Mom

I hope you are well. I am doing fine. At this moment I am sitting at the table, writing this letter, and listening to my new Sony WALKMAN. I Bet I have a wide grin on my face. Thank you for sending the extra money. You can think of this as my Birthday present. I didn't realize how much I had missed my music. This was the best $22.00 you have spent in a while. I had a wonderful visit Saturday. It was so good to see Paul & Marlon. Bob & Shelley came also. I don't know what Bob did to get Shelley to come — she is always tired — working all week & taking care of her flower garden! I sure miss you & Georgia — I hope you can come this Saturday! I still have $50.00 left, that should last me 2 weeks. Paul told me about some kind of lost ($200.00) associated with my child support case. It must be court cost. Don't work to hard! I miss you & love you VERY much

P.S. Thanks Again for the Radio — She's 3!
— I hope you Remembered to call Red Saturday!

3-29-02

Hello Mom
        HAPPY EASTER
I Hope you have been doing Fine this week!
I know you aren't used to working a full
week yet & I don't know If I will be
Seeing you Tomorrow, or not. I haven't called
Georgia yet. I'll call her this afternoon.
I was so sore yesterday, that I didn't want
to get out of Bed. I went out on the yard
Wednesday afternoon, I walked 4 miles,
As fast As I could walk, thats pretty Fast.
I Also did some Push-ups. I enjoyed It
Very much. It was A Beautiful afternoon,
and I put my headphones on, and took off
walking. I had to work Thursday, so
I had to Tough it out & set up. I was glad
to get off early - (About 11:00 pm). I went
to Bed to Read - and ended up sleeping until
6:00 pm. I got my Books From Janaya
and Brad on the same day - Wednesday.
Janaya Sent me 2 more - But Brad Surprised
me, with the whole "AREA 51" Series - He
Had Already Sent me one of them, & He
Sent me the other 5. Yes I called & Thanked
Him
        I LOVE YOU &
            DAVE

MAY 1, 2002

Good Morning George

I hope your back is Better. Maybe
that new Medicine will work well, for you.
The main thing you have to do is realize,
that, for a month or 2, At least, you will
have to be especially careful. Don't
overdo it, don't lift anything, that you
don't absolutely have to, and don't stay in
uncomfortable positions, for very long at
one time.
I hope Rodney & Uncle Benny got all
the Bugs worked out of the truck, in time,
for Rodney to leave today.
I will be forever grateful to you, for everything,
you have done to help me, while I have been
incarcerated. You have helped me in so many
ways. Thank you for calling Bob, and
for thinking of Debbie & Bear. He
will get Bear's Medicine as soon as he
feels Better. Hopefully, they won't hold
me back, from going to Work Release, very
long. I am the only Electrician they
have, in outside Maintenance, Right Now.
Please take Extra CARE with your BACK!
I'll call you TodAy!

I Love You WADE!

Happy Pre - Mother's DAY!

123

May 1, 2002

Good Morning Mom

Well, I don't feel 40 years old! I Guess
It is better, than feeling older, than my years!
You know how I always say, The lord works
in mysterious ways. Here is one more
example. You are aware, of how, I used to
refuse, to work on my birthday. I put in my
sick-call request, to go to the Nurse, and get
my weekly Sinus Medicine. It can take, from
2 - 7 days, to get put on Sick-call, from
the time you put in a request. I put my
request in Sunday, I am laid in all day,
for Sick-call. That means I don't have to
go to work. I told you, that I don't buy
Ice cream on the store, during the week.
I save that for a treat, during Visitation. I am
going to splurge today - since Monday &
Wednesday are store days out here.
I can't have a birthday cake & Ice Cream,
but I can have a pint of Ice Cream &
an apple or cherry pie (Individual Pastry).
It could be alot worse, Plus I will
get to talk to George in this Afternoon -
Thank you for the $100.00 - I was down to
$1.35. I know you are going to be
finished, with your Job, on May 10th.

4-5-02

Good Morning Mom

It's Friday morning, and since my
Boss didn't come get me for work, I
thought It would be a good time to
write Some Letters. My Boss told me
Wednesday, that he put me up for a
job change. After learning that, and
talking to Georgia, I put in a request, to
talk with mis Woods. Mis. Woods is the
ClassificAtion lady. I should go up IN front
of the classification Board Tuesday, The 9th.
Hopefully, after talking to the Child support
Investigator, mis woods will let me have
my 1-B Trusty, Even if they dont get Verification,
By Tuesday. Then I can put in my APPlication
for work - Release & "309", and ride cowboy
on the Beef-Herd until Walk-Release comes
to get me. I talked to my friend yesterday
Afternoon, And he told me the only person,
they were putting A hold on, in the Beef-
Herd, was the person who shoed the horses.
I probably wont get to talk to her Monday,
But I will learn something on Tuesday,
either way. Thank you for the money,
I haven't gotten it yet, but it will get here
Before I run out.

I'm glad you are going to take
care of Bear's Heart worm Medicine.
It would devastate me, if something
happened to him, while I am locked up.
I have been the only constant in his life,
now he doesn't know what happened to me,
or where I have gone. Debbie said
that he still searches for me, every time
some one pulls up, at the house. It
took her forever to get him to eat
properly. It is comforting that he has
accepted her so well.
I am thankful, that you have a job,
that pays you so well, It is even better,
that you don't have to drive. I believe,
It will work out, that I will be in a work-
release, about the time your Job runs out.
That way you can go spend some time,
with Red, without worrying so much, about
money. I missed being with you this
past week-end, but hopefully, I'll get to see you
soon. I love you very much —

WADE

(2)

Hello George

I hope you will read mom's letter also, because it's getting dark. I'll have to be short & sweet, before the Sun goes down. I didn't call Rodney this week-end, figured I would let it get closer to christmas. ~~That is~~ The last thing I want, is for him to feel uncomfortable, when he looks at his phone bill. This is the last week, of my 30 day waiting period. I wish you or mom, would call the Visitation office, and remind them. Next month I want my 2 regular Visitations. I am going to get very upset if I cant, because some Idiot hasn't done her, or his, Job. Debbie called yesterday the lady she talked to, told her she was busy, and didn't have time to check on it — to call her back that B.S. will not work — I have decided I want to find some land between Heber & Batesville. I have also figured out your surprise, I know Its mean to make you wait 2 years — If you really want to know, I will probably break down —

I love you Georgia,

WADE

P.S. Give uncle Benny A Hug
& remind mom to bring a few

☆ She may want to bring a money
order, too — It's up to her.

Sun 6-2-02

Hello Mom & Red!

I am combining your Letters. I don't want to ~~write it~~ write this info Twice!
Thanks for your Letters & E-Mails.
Red, I am glad that you Just forgot to order those books. I didn't want you to have paid for them, and them be lost somewhere.

I had 2 days off this week - Wednesday & Saturday. I will get one day off Next week. My work schedule will work like that, until I leave for Work-Release. I Should get Interviewed (They call it screened) during the First part of this month. After I have been screened, and approved, it shouldn't take a month after that. I Should be at a Work-Release center, by no later than August. August 9th will be a year & I figure the next year will go by a lot faster. I will be working at a real Job, making money, and getting one week-end a month at home. My week-end in December may not be around Christmas, but it will be close enough. I know I have a cushy Job now, but I am still impatient, to get to Work-Release —

I had a very good Visit SaTurday.
Debbie's mom, and a friend of hers,
brought Debbie, and dropped her off.
They went shopping in Pine Bluff, and
Picked her up at 3:00 Pm. We had 3½
hours to visit. She is looking alot better.
She has gained about 5 lbs. After my
Visit, I decided my shoulder WAS ready for
a tost Run. I Started early, since the
Handball court WAS empty, and I could
get in A little practice. My Shoulder
didn't Bother me, near as much as my
extra 25 lbs. I Still did alright for
a FAt Boy, HAD that hasn't played since the
early 80'S. I won 1 and lost 3. Yes
the lAST Three were against good PlAyers.
I got A very good sweaty work out — ThATs
whAT I wanted. I think I will Spend the
money, for a pair of tennis shoes, when my
next money gets here — Remember my BooTS —
thAts what I played IN. I plAn on plAying
Again this Afternoon, to work out the
StiffNess! I figure I CAN get BACK in
fair shape, in the next 6–8 weeks!
I wANt to be in Better shape for work — Released,
I Love + miss you All very Much — ooo

3-18-02

— Give Benny A Hug!

Hello George

I Hope you and uncle Benny are
Doing Good, I Think I made a wise
choice on my Radio — not only WAS It
$2.50 cheaper, but It uses only 1 AA
BAttery Instead of 2 AAA, like the
AIWA. A Few guys have told me that the
Sony will pick up more STATions Also.
   I don't Know Anything About the INLINE
6 cylinder motor. AS A Rule, 6 Cylinders
lAst a long Time — They don't develop RPM'S AS A.
They Also deliver a lot of Torque — for Towing.
Plus 275 HP's more than my '97
350 Put out — That Should Be a good
combination. The main Thing IS the
fact that I know How many SAFety
features they HAVe — Remember how hard
I hit that Tree in my '97 — Without my
SeatBelt, You made a very wise choice.
I Am mailing you a Visitation form + LANDon
one Also. I know It won't Be IN time
for Him to come thIS SAturday, But If
He Hurries + Gets It sent BACK — He cAN
come next Time! I'll CAll you Friday
ThAnKS for EVERything — I Hope to see you
SATurday — I miss you + mom.

Front
My Truck

Hello George

Didn't want to pass up a Chance
to say Thank you. I appreciate
every thing you do, probably more than
you understand. I'll see you and
Uncle Benny soon —

Have a Good Day

I love you

Wade

131

Good Morning George'

Just when I think I will never be
able to show you how much I Appreciate
every thing you have done, you do something
else, That never fails, to make me feel
like the luckiest person on Earth!
Some people don't even get the wonderful
feeling of 1 mother's unconditional Love,
And God has blessed me with three —
even though he has tAken one from me,
I am still one of the richest and most Blessed
people ever! I don't mean to sound,
like I am not AwAre of, — and appreciate,
how much my mother loves me —
But she Is my Mother. When I think
of the pain, and stress that I have brought
upon both of you, It makes me Cry!
I hope to see you soon. I love
Very Much —

WADE

3-29-02

Hello George

HAPPY EASTER

I hope you aren't wearing yourself
down, Working Too Hard on these taxes!
How Is your new Truck Working out?
I hope you like IT. Tell Rodney not
To Worry About Me, that much. If he
cAme to visit, Before he was finished,
his body would be here, but not his heart + mind
Do you think we might could get him to
give you a SATurdAy Morning off —
After he is through with his Truck, of Course
I'm going to cut this short so I can
get it in the mail, on the wAy to Chow.
It's almost 10:00 Am — They ARe LiAble
to CAll Chow Any minute — Give uncle
Benny A Hug —
I Love you —

1-19-03

Hello Hayley

I'm glad you made It home Safely.
Did you Enjoy your Trip? I hope so!
It was gleat to see you, for a whole
weekend. I hope I get to see
you and your family, on at least
one more of my weekends, Before
I get out for good. I don't want a
whole year to go By, without Seeing
you again. Please be the sweet
young lady, that I know you are.
Keep trying hard in school, and help
your Mom, as much as you CAN.
I love you very much HAyley.

Love & Kisses
uncle WADE

P.S. I would like
To Hear From
you, every Now
and then.

134

SundAy 6-2-02

Hello HAyley

Thank you for your Letter, and
your pretty drawing. I glad you
like your neckLAce. The Main thing Is
for you to Remember How much your
uncle Wade Loves you & YOUR Mom
SAid that you Picked up the GAme,
of Soft bAll, very Quickly. I knew you would.
You Are a Spunky, enersetic young
Lady. Your Mom Said that your bAby
brother wAs getting as fAt, As a PiG.
That means he Is good and healthy &
I hope you have a Wonderful Summer, and
a SAfe one. I think I may get to See
you Soon — Be a good Girl —

I MISS you and I Love you
vERy much &&&

                    uncle WADE

135

①   FridAy 6-14-02

Hello Mom, & Red

    Yes, you two ARe going to have to share a letter. I don't want to write all this down twice. I got Both letters. The letter with the money order, I recieved yesterday, Thank you. I thought that WAS cute, that JAKe wanted to keep his letter pprivate. I hope the little pistol, didn't have any trouble, reading my hand writing. Thank you For the Computer Pictures. Boy, you woren't Kidding, about CARSon being a little butter bAll. When are ya'll coming to ARKAWSAS? ARE JAKe and bAyley coming to see me Also? What are you going to do with CARSon while you come visit? What Do you cAll him, CARSon or CARSon Wade? I got the paper, telling me that Landon is Approved, to Visit. Before ya'll Come, Please remember, to CALL the Visitation office, and make sure you are on the list! He, (LAndon) and Geosgia, Rodney might Come with them, ARe going to Come visit soon. I to Remember to tell Geosgia, that he IS Approved, when I CAll this Afternoon. I didn't get to talk to her, last Friday, they were gone t Indianapolis, Indiana.

②

Rodney had a CAR Show there.
He did good. He got another award.
I called him Monday night. I will try
and get ahold of Brad, This Afternoon.
I hope you Remembered to call Him o
I still don't know which work Release,
I will go to. I did find out, that Pine Bluff
doesn't come and screen Applicants in Person.
They Just come get you. I asked Brad
to check on the one in Springdale. He
can call and find out all the Information.
It's small, but the Jobs are good, and so
is the Pay. The only negative thing, Is,
that it is so far away, from every one else.
I will just be glad, to be back making
money o I have from 18-21 months left,
If I can save a minimum, of $500.ºº a month,
I should have between, $9,000ºº & $11,000ºº.
I should be able to pay cash for a truck, and
have some left over. Robbie said he could
help me find one. I should be able to get
a used mazda 4x4 for less than $10,000.
I will need something, dependable, good on GAS,
and 4x4, I won't care what it looks like,
or how fast it runs. I will need it to run alot
of miles, as cheap as possible. The 4x4 will
Be a must o   I Miss you & Love you
Both very much ooo
                    Wade

Sunday 9-22-02

Hello Sis

I don't Know If Mom is still There,
If she is, she can read this also. I hope
I hope things have smoothed out, for you.
I think It WAS a wise decision for Robbie,
to go to Finance School. I told him that a
long time ago. As A Finance person, he
Will make money, on the contracting of all the Sales.
He will Also be out of the Politics of Management.
    I guess Mom has told you of my Job, It was
tough. It WAS very hot and Physically demanding. I
have lost between 5 + 10 Pounds, but More Important,
I have gotten aloT of my stamina Back. Wednesday
Morning I had a very heated ARgument, With the
Free-world Black man, that I worked with. Tuesday
Afternoon, my Boss told me to come into work 2 hours
early (at 5:00 Am), I WAS to hang Clean shirts on the
line. He tried to tell me to set to work on the
mats. I told him to leave me alone, he wasn't my
Boss, and I knew, what I WAS supposed to do.
He got in my fACe, and I Instantly reacted. He is
not in JAil, so he has nothing to lose, except his Job
Very Quickly, another Inmate (BlACk) talked him
down. As he left, he Said he would get me.
At 4:00 Am, I went to the mat ARea to go to

138

I told him he had no say so, in where
I worked. I realized real quick, that I
WAS about to lose Control, And hit him.
I told him he WAS very lucky, that, I WAS
in JAil, and couldn't Afford to beat his
Ass. I turned around and WAlked off.
I went to the Bosses Office. They ARRived about
7:15 Am. I told them what had hAppened, and.
Rf they didn't handle the Situation, that I would.
I was not putting up with someone threatening
me! The boss talked to both of us. Told us to
do our job, and leave each other alone. To not
even speak to each other. The next day they
moved me to a Janitorial Job. The lord works in
Mysterious WAys. He tested me, I pAssed, He
rewArded me. I like my new Job. I have
a lot of different responsibilities, and time goes
by very quickly. I do a lot of WAlking, but I
ordered me a pair f Doc MArten Work Boots.
They were 109.00 -minus a 10% discount. I wiy
have to leave them at work, in my locker. They
should be very comfortable. I make 7.00/HR,
and get any where from 40, to 55 hrs. My normal
HRS. are from 17:00am to 3:30am.

③

I had 2 visits Saturday. Bob and Debbie came first, and Georgia and Rodney came at 2:30 P.M. I really enjoyed seeing Georgia, and Rodney. I tried to call, but your Phone doesn't cooperate any more. I can't talk to you, so Please keep sending me copies of your e-mails. Tell Hayley and Jake how much I miss & love Them. If Mom is still There, She knows How much I love Her, Just Give her a Kiss for me. Mom, Please be extra careful, not to let the Baby Distract you while you're driving. I can't have anything happen to either one of you 6 Well, I am going to go Take a Shower, & Shave, and get ready for church. I love and miss you All very much b/b Yes, Robbie, even you — #8

<u>Hello JAKE!</u>

I hope you have been having
fun playing baseball. You sure
do look sharp in the pictures
you sent me. The pictures of you
playing baseball. I hope you
and your friends, have a good place
to play, close to your houses. Hopefully,
you will be coming to see me soon.
You CAN tell me all about it then.
Bob has left to go to the big
Indian Dance. It is called the
Sun Dance. It is a very Big thing.
It last about a week. It is a Dance
that praises God, and all he Gives us
through the Sun. Not everyone Dances.
The Dancers will Dance Night and Day,
for 4 days. The Dancers Don't
Eat or Drink for the whole 4 days.
Then Everyone Joins the Dancers in a feast.
Summer after Next, Maybe your Mom,
will let you go with me and Bob,
to a real Sundance, Ask you Mom,
She might find you a book on Native
American Dances. I hope to see you

Sunday 6-2-02

Hello Jake

Thank you for your drawing. I hope you
like your necklace. It is a real Indian
Arrow head. The small ones, like that
one were mostly used for Ceremonies.
They are called Bird Points, But real
Arrow heads, for Shooting Birds, were
Blunt + rounded instead of Sharp Pointed,

Bird Point

regular Hunting Point

That way they would Knock a Bird down,
But were less likely to Be damaged, or
lost in the Trunk of A Tree.
    Your Mom told Me you did real
Well in Baseball, I knew you would
get over being hit in the nose, by that Ball.
I hope you have a very fun Summer.
I may get to see ya'll Soon - Be Careful
and Stay Safe -

        I Love you Very Much

        Uncle Wads

142

Friday 6-14-02

Hello Hayley

How are you? I hope you are doing
as well, As you look in you pictures.
From those pictures you sent me, it looks
like you are rapidly becoming, a Beautiful
young Lady. If you are careful, not
to act without thinking, you'll be Surprised
how easy it will be, to keep from doing things,
you will be ashamed of later. Always
keep your head up, and be very proud of
who you are. You are very special, there
is not another person like you.
I am glad that you enjoyed Softball.
It is Always good to broaden your experiences
in life. That is the way you find out what
you like and what you don't. I hope
yall are enjoying your Summer to the fullest.
I hope to get to See you Soon, and you
can tell Me all about it. Help your mom
and your Mimi - So you can all Have fun.
I miss you and love you very much.

Uncle WADE

Thursday June 27, 2002

Hello JAKE

I Hope my Little Buddy is doing Well.
ARE you having a fun Summer? I'm
Sorry we didn't get to visit, when you CAME
to Arkansas. I think they will have every
thing Straightened out, by the time you come
Back, I hope you have a SAFE 4th of July
Holiday. Be careful with those Fireworks!
Bob got Back from the Indian Sun
Dance, on Sunday. He was very tired.
Did you have your Mom find you some
Information, on The Sun Dance? I am
almost ½ done being in Jail. I only
have to be away from ya'll, for one more Summer.
Be A Good Boy. I'll See you Soon.
I Love you Very much bbb

Uncle Wade.

5-20-02

Happy Birthday Jake

I hope you had A Great Birthday. Mimi will Be Bringing your present with her. I hope you like it. I didn't Buy it, I found it, and it is hand made afterward. I'm Sorry we didn't get to talk long, because you were in the bath tub. I will be calling this week end, we can talk some more then. I hope you Are having fun playing Baseball. You will be out of school for Summer Vacation Soon, I hope you have a fun Summer. We have this Summer and one more, before we can Start some Serious fishing. It will Be over Before you know it, And I'll Be Home — Be a Good Boy This Summer — I miss youd

I Love you very Much Jake

Uncle Wade

Begining Balance

				$55.72
Task No.	Date	Task	Comment	Amount
20635	9/3/2002 6:37:50 PM	Sale		($14.59)
21101	9/6/2002 8:21:04 PM	Sale		($10.87)
21102	9/6/2002 8:21:43 PM	Sale		($2.64)
21171	9/9/2002 8:33:54 AM	Automated Payment	START DATE 9/03/02 CHARGE 6 DAY	($90.00)
21472	9/10/2002 9:43:52 AM	Automated Payment	RENT FOR 9/9-15/02	($105.00)
21564	9/10/2002 9:44:52 AM	Automated Payment	UNIFORMS FOR 9/9-15/02	($7.00)
21747	9/10/2002 6:05:40 PM	Sale		($8.00)
22251	9/13/2002 6:34:21 PM	Sale		($15.54)
22401	9/16/2002 4:09:53 PM	Automated Payment	RENT FOR 9/16-22/02	($105.00)
22493	9/16/2002 4:10:44 PM	Automated Payment	UNIFORM FOR 9/16-22/02	($7.00)
22683	9/17/2002 9:46:50 AM	ROA	Work Release Pay	$158.84
22988	9/17/2002 8:12:24 PM	Sale		($14.59)
23382	9/20/2002 7:21:28 PM	Sale		($9.88)
23479	9/23/2002 10:47:51 AM	Automated Payment	RENT CHARGE 9/23-29/02	($105.00)
23570	9/23/2002 10:50:13 AM	Automated Payment	UNIFORM CHARGE FOR 9/23-29/02	($7.00)
23783	9/24/2002 9:39:13 AM	ROA	Work Release Pay	$300.28
24000	9/24/2002 7:45:55 PM	Sale		($19.29)
24342	9/27/2002 6:34:41 PM	Sale		($5.33)
24464	9/30/2002 1:06:06 PM	Automated Payment	RENT FOR 09/30-10/6/02	($105.00)
24554	9/30/2002 1:07:32 PM	Automated Payment	Work Release Uniforms	($7.00)

Ending Balance

				($123.89)

Begining Balance

$835.20

Task No.	Date	Task	Comment	Amount
82256	3/3/03 12:46:57 PM	Automated Payment	RENT FOR 3/3-9/03	($105.00)
82341	3/3/03 12:47:35 PM	Automated Payment	UNIFORM FOR 3/3-9/03	($7.00)
82560	3/4/03 10:12:30 AM	ROA	Work Release Pay	$322.05
82756	3/4/03 6:00:32 PM	Sale		($14.50)
83103	3/6/03 4:14:25 PM	Group Withdrawal		($30.00)
83401	3/10/03 12:02:51 PM	Automated Payment	RENT FOR 3/10-16/03	($105.00)
83485	3/10/03 12:06:05 PM	Automated Payment	UNIFORMS FOR 3/10-16/03	($7.00)
83788	3/11/03 2:01:19 PM	ROA	Work Release Pay	$190.59
83872	3/11/03 6:00:25 PM	Sale		($22.45)
84173	3/13/03 2:54:48 PM	Group Withdrawal		($30.00)
84524	3/17/03 9:32:50 AM	Automated Payment	RENT - 3/17-23/03	($105.00)
84608	3/17/03 9:33:21 AM	Automated Payment	3/17-23/03	($7.00)
84731	3/18/03 9:11:24 AM	ROA	Work Release Pay	$213.75
84924	3/18/03 6:15:06 PM	Sale		($21.90)
85185	3/20/03 1:52:08 PM	Group Withdrawal		($30.00)
85481	3/24/03 10:12:14 AM	Automated Payment	RENT 3/24/03 TO 3/30/03	($105.00)
85566	3/24/03 10:13:01 AM	Automated Payment	UNIFORMS 3/24/03 TO 3/30/03	($7.00)
85943	3/25/03 3:17:11 PM	ROA	Work Release Pay	$212.53
85984	3/25/03 5:47:54 PM	Sale		($22.39)
86113	3/27/03 9:30:17 AM	Group Withdrawal		($30.00)

Ending Balance

$1,124.88

RULES AND REGULATIONS
WORK RELEASE WEEKEND FURLOUGH
RULES GOVERNING CONDUCT WHILE ON WEEKEND FURLOUGH
NO INMATE RELEASED ON WEEKEND FURLOUGH SHALL:

Dec. 6, 2001

1. Leave the State of Arkansas for any purpose under any circumstances;
2. Leave the county to which he/she was furloughed except for travel to the county and return travel to the unit/center without the expressed written consent and approval of the Warden/Center Supervisor;
3. Possess of consume any alcoholic beverages;
4. Visit any place of business where alcoholic beverages are the major items sold or consumed;
5. Violate any Federal, State, County or Municipal laws;
6. Any inmate on furlough will NOT operate any motor vehicle under any circumstances.
7. Possess or consume any drugs other than those prescribed for him/her by a licensed physician. In the event the inmate requires medical attention outside a Department facility and for which a prescription is written, he/she will request the medical person who issues the prescription to call the Unit/Center and inform them of this medical treatment to include any needed prescription. In the event the medical person is unable or unwilling to notify the Unit/Center and furnish all pertinent medical information;
8. Will not identify the Department of Correction as the responsible authority for any cost incurred for health services provided while on furlough. The responsibility for costs incurred due to medical treatment rendered while on furlough will be borne by the inmate or insurance/source other than the Department Of Correction. If the health condition of the inmate is in need of emergency attention, either the inmate or sponsor will make immediate notification to the Warden/Center Supervisor. Arrangements will then be initiated to meet this need under Department Of Correction procedures;
). Violate any Department Of Correction rules and regulations.

/eekend furloughs begin on FRIDAY at 5:00 p.m. and end on SUNDAY at 5:00 Inmate must be returned to Unit prior to 5:00 p.m. on the last day of his ugh.

Memories
for
life...
Mom
Your The
Worlds
Greatest

<u>Mother,</u>

The lord sent
a bit of heaven
when he gave me You.
He Knew You
Would always care
and always be true.
You have made my life
So beautiful
for me to see,
You have given hope
when things
looked hopelessly...

...Now each tomorrow
is a brighter day
for me to see,
and I want to
thank You lord
for Sending
<u>My Mom to me</u>!
<u>Love</u>

I love you Totally!!!
Wade

Office of the Sheriff

BENTON COUNTY SHERIFF'S OFFICE
DETENTION FACILITY

DATE: 10-3-01

CIRCLE ONE: GRIEVANCE   REQUEST   (MEDICAL)

NATURE: _Lower Back Intur_

INMATE NAME: _Loudon Wade Dilliday_   DOB _May 1962_   CELL BLOCK _D-149_

WRITTEN EXPLANATION: _I need something to ease my lower back Pain - Especially at Bedtime. You have given me Ibuprofen in the past. It helps!_

RECEIVED BY: _Culp_   DATE _10-3-01_   TIME _1947_

RESPONSE: _Will see nurse_

DATE: _10401_   TIME: _0510_   BY: _M Norman_

PHONE CALLS

Phone Calls can be accessed through the Inmate Phone System. Additions and deletions to this list should be forwarded to the Shift Commander, Capt. S. O'Neal.

Attorneys should be specifically designated as attorneys to better facilitate legal calls.

GRAPHIC ARTS

PROGRAM MANAGER – GARY THOMAS

The Graphic Arts Industry was formed to provide inmates with training in a marketable skill while offering tax-supported agencies and non-profit organizations quality printing at minimal cost.

There are six basic areas in Graphic Arts Industry consisting of the following: Printing Presses, Photo lab, Stripping Area, Cutting Area, Padding Area, and the Collate area.

FURNITURE INDUSTRY

PROGRAM MANAGER – TIM LOWERY

The Furniture Industry is a very complex and extensive service responsible for the design, manufacture, and packaging of furniture products. The process begins with a customer order. If the product is a special order, a team of inmates is assigned to layout, design, and draw specifications for the product before production starts. The lumber is milled and cut, then sent to the assembly area. There, the parts are assembled and made ready for sanding and the final finish. Once the finish is applied, the product is inspected and packed for transfer to the 145th Street Warehouse. Inmates in this program are also afforded marketable skills upon spending ample time in this program.

YOUR ADDRESS IS:

Name/ ADC# / BKS#
Wrightsville Unit
P.O. Box 1000
Wrightsville, AR 72183-1000

WRIGHTSVILLE UNIT
ORIENTATION INFORMATION

Warden – Kay Howell
Asst. Warden – Vacant
Chief Security Officer- John Whaley
Building Captain – Carl Stout
Field Major – Robert Perry
Institutional Parole Officer- M. Howard
Recreation Supervisor – Tommy Curtner
Boot Camp Administrator – T. Rochelle
Commissary Manger – Suzie Rhodes

Classification Officer – L. Marshall
Records Supervisor – Lynette James
Senior Chaplain – Gary Cox
Building Captain – Steven O'Neal
Grievance Officer – Tina Hamilton
Mailroom Supervisor- Daisy Lee
Visitation Clerk – Ms. Parker
Infirmary Manager- Sharon Rogers
School Principal – Fred Johnson

PRE-RELEASE PROGRAM

PROGRAM COORDINATOR – BRUCE HART

The Pre-Release program, located in 17 barracks, was established at the Wrightsville Unit with three main goals:

1. Make information, counseling and assistance in release planning available to inmates.

2. Provide each inmate an opportunity, in a non-threatening situation, to discuss problems and anxieties relating to his release and future adjustment.

3. Provide a system of re-orientation, through motivational training, to assist the inmate in his reintegration into "free-world" society and thereby reduce recidivism.

The Wrightsville Unit Pre-Release program includes lectures and discussions that address the concerns of the soon to be released inmate. Also, individual counseling focuses on each inmate's particular needs.

SCHOOL

PRINCIPAL – FRED JOHNSON

The Wrightsville Unit School starts teaching at the elementary level and it continues through the GED program. The school is broken down in levels instead of grades, and students are promoted as they master subjects at each level.

PHONE CALLS

Phone Calls can be accessed through the Inmate Phone System. Additions and deletions to this list should be forwarded to the Shift Commander, Capt. S. O'Neal.

Attorneys should be specifically designated as attorneys to better facilitate legal calls.

GRAPHIC ARTS

PROGRAM MANAGER – GARY THOMAS

The Graphic Arts Industry was formed to provide inmates with training in a marketable skill while offering tax-supported agencies and non-profit organizations quality printing at minimal cost.

There are six basic areas in Graphic Arts Industry consisting of the following: Printing Presses, Photo lab, Stripping Area, Cutting Area, Padding Area, and the Collate area.

FURNITURE INDUSTRY

PROGRAM MANAGER – TIM LOWERY

The Furniture Industry is a very complex and extensive service responsible for the design, manufacture, and packaging of furniture products. The process begins with a customer order. If the product is a special order, a team of inmates is assigned to layout, design, and draw specifications for the product before production starts. The lumber is milled and cut, then sent to the assembly area. There, the parts are assembled and made ready for sanding and the final finish. Once the finish is applied, the product is inspected and packed for transfer to the 145th Street Warehouse. Inmates in this program are also afforded marketable skills upon spending ample time in this program.

YOUR ADDRESS IS:

Name/ ADC# / BKS#
Wrightsville Unit
P.O. Box 1000
Wrightsville, AR 72183-1000

WRIGHTSVILLE UNIT
ORIENTATION INFORMATION

Warden – Kay Howell
Asst. Warden – Vacant
Chief Security Officer- John Whaley
Building Captain – Carl Stout
Field Major – Robert Perry
Institutional Parole Officer- M. Howard
Recreation Supervisor – Tommy Curtner
Boot Camp Administrator – T. Rochelle
Commissary Manger – Suzie Rhodes

Classification Officer – L. Marshall
Records Supervisor – Lynette James
Senior Chaplain – Gary Cox
Building Captain – Steven O'Neal
Grievance Officer – Tina Hamilton
Mailroom Supervisor- Daisy Lee
Visitation Clerk – Ms. Parker
Infirmary Manager- Sharon Rogers
School Principal – Fred Johnson

PRE-RELEASE PROGRAM

PROGRAM COORDINATOR – BRUCE HART

The Pre-Release program, located in 17 barracks, was established at the Wrightsville Unit with three main goals:

1. Make information, counseling and assistance in release planning available to inmates.

2. Provide each inmate an opportunity, in a non-threatening situation, to discuss problems and anxieties relating to his release and future adjustment.

3. Provide a system of re-orientation, through motivational training, to assist the inmate in his reintegration into "free-world" society and thereby reduce recidivism.

The Wrightsville Unit Pre-Release program includes lectures and discussions that address the concerns of the soon to be released inmate. Also, individual counseling focuses on each inmate's particular needs.

SCHOOL

PRINCIPAL – FRED JOHNSON

The Wrightsville Unit School starts teaching at the elementary level and it continues through the GED program. The school is broken down in levels instead of grades, and students are promoted as they master subjects at each level.